MONEY MORON
TO MONEY MAGNET

Attract Wealth and
Upgrade Your Financial Future Instantly

Ryan Baily

10-10-10
Publishing

Money Moron to Money Magnet:
Attract Wealth and Upgrade Your Financial Future Instantly
Baily, Ryan

ISBN: 978-1-77277-260-9

Published by:
10-10-10 Publishing
Markham, Ontario

First 10-10-10 Publishing paperback edition January 2019

Table of Contents

*This book is dedicated to anyone
who feels they can be and do more!*

Foreword

You are living in an interesting time right now. There is so much uncertainty all over the world. Job security is at its lowest, employer funded pensions are a thing of the past, and government and educational systems are hard pressed to find a solution. The national debt in Canada is skyrocketing and a recent statistic shows that over 50% of the population is in financial hardship. The numbers in the United States are even worse. It doesn't take a rocket scientist to realize a change is in order.

If you're a person who is financially strained or is already well off, this book is for you. Ryan Baily has laid out basic universal concepts that you can learn from, and that can redirect you towards a healthier and wealthier life.

I met Ryan at one of my public speaking seminars and was instantly impressed with his dedication to learning. He has a strong personality and above all else is dedicated to changing the financial landscape. I can tell he genuinely cares and has put all of his ideas within this book for you to learn from.

So, be prepared to be rescued from the sea of sameness and escape the rat race which is your finances. Make your stride towards the success you desire and deserve. I have helped Ryan and he is there to help you. Then, in turn, as you thrive, pass on these amazing concepts and ideas to a new generation of students. Enjoy and learn from this book. The ideas in it can work for you, so you don't have to work yourself.

Raymond Aaron
New York Times Bestselling Author

Acknowledgements

First off, I would like to thank my loving wife, **Lisetty Sandoval**. You are the shining light in my life. We've gone through ups and downs, but we've created the family that we both dreamed of. You've supported me whenever I needed, and I'll continue to support you for the rest of my life.

Huge thanks to my publisher **Raymond Aaron**. Your motivation and training are what motivates me to do more. It's because of you and your teachings that this book exists.

I'd like to thank the one of the greatest speakers out there, **Tony Robbins**. We met only briefly at one of your seminars in Toronto and I was blown away. Your devotion and commitment to helping people achieve more moved me in the direction to serve others. It's your insights and techniques that really pushed me to write this book, and made me the man I am today.

To my first motivational sales trainer, **Larry Galbo**. At times, your toughness and energy are what pushed me to excel for excellence. All your training and talks, all those years, helped me in life and are the real reason I now have an unstoppable attitude.

To the last boss I ever had, **Fikret Sukru**. You took a chance on me during a down time in my life. I learned a lot during our many talks, which were an inspiration for what a true leader should be.

To an old sales manager, **Shail Silver**. Your youth and energy inspire me to keep moving. You've accomplished a lot at a young age, and our talks back in the day helped me to keep focused and aiming for the prize.

To the host of the TV show, *Till Debt Do Us Part*, **Gail Vaz-Oxlade**. It's because of you and your push on national television that really motivated me to change my financial ways. I learned a lot during our short time, and your concepts continue to resonate with me till today.

To my acting professor, **John Bourgeois,** from Humber College. You changed the way I view human interaction and what it means to be in touch with myself. Your training and motivation not only helped in my career but motivated me to learn and be more.

To my speed reading and memory coach, **Jim Kwik**. Your insights and techniques truly opened my mind to a new world of knowledge. Your programs transformed me and my family to strive to be super learners. Thank you.

To the one woman who never gave up hope on me; my grandmother, **Edyth Baily**. You left this world recently, and I will never forget you. Even when I was down as a child, you were there to always bring me up and show me the best I could be.

Act 1

Why Should You Change???

Chapter 1
Under the Bridge

"As long as poverty, injustice, and gross inequality persist in our world, none of us can truly rest."
– Nelson Mandela

There I was, lying under the bridge—cold, wet, and scared—nothing, and no one around me, except for dirt and garbage. I had probably been there for 3 or 4 days, but I was homeless and only 14 years old. My only belongings were a backpack full of clothes, a toothbrush, toothpaste, and a comb. All I could wonder was how I got here and how I could go so low. Was life meant to be like this???

A few days earlier, I had a falling out with my mother after one of our many fights of my rebellious youth, but this time things quickly escalated out of hand, and I left for good.

Initially, a friend of mine took me in. His parents allowed it and were very supportive; they knew my home was broken and not currently safe. I was able to stay there a few days. Unfortunately, it was nearing the beginning of the school year, and that friend didn't really like the idea of me staying at his house for too long. To be honest, I don't really blame him, as I would have felt the same way—so he asked me to leave. With his parents doubting my choice and not knowing that I truly had nowhere to go, I obliged and left quietly.

Unfortunately, I had burned bridges with my uncle and grandmother on another incident a few years earlier, so my choices were limited. I ended up making camp underneath a train bridge in Guelph, Ontario, not too far from my home, near the downtown core. Surprisingly, my initial thoughts were actually positive. This was the first time I was independent and on my own! A similar feeling, I suppose, of a college or university student moving into a dorm for the first time and being finally free from mom and dad's influence. I was free and going to take on the world! That feeling was short-lived.

I used the clothes in my backpack as a blanket at night, as it was early September, and the nights were getting cold. I was lucky to find bread that was about 2 days old, lying outside a nearby apartment building, which kept me from starving. At night, I remember staring up at the stars while it rained, with thunder and lightning going on, and I prayed to God: I did not want to be in this position; I was better than this; and I was going do something, and be somebody. At the time, I didn't know what or how, but that prayer would come true—way, way, way, waaayyyy down the road—and become somebody, I did.

From what I remember, my early childhood was a pretty happy time. My parents showed slight affection. My mother was a stay-at-home mom, and my father was a janitor at a tool and die factory. They bought me lots of toys and gifts at Christmas and Easter. I got all dressed up like all the other kids and went out on Halloween and got lots of candy. Like most children, I was completely oblivious to the world around me. Sure, my mom would slap me from time to time as punishment, but I figured that was normal. It wasn't until 8 or 9 years of age that I started to figure out the world I was being raised in.

Kids in school would pick on me about my parents. Even friends I did have weren't allowed to sleep over at my house because their parents wouldn't let them. At first, I didn't understand, but I did notice there was something different about my parents compared to all the other parents. At that age, all I thought was that sure, they talked a little different, dressed a little different, but hey, they're my parents, and I was supposed to do what they say, learn from them, and respect them... right?? Now, by today's standards, both my parents are placed in the category of mentally handicapped or mentally challenged. When I was around the age of 8, my father got laid off from his janitor job, and they relied solely on social assistance/welfare and charity to survive, and they still do to this day.

I imagine my parents did the best they could with what they had, and with what they knew. The only difficult part was when my intelligence level reached theirs by about the age of 12. It became very hard to respect and listen to my parents when they were unable to mentor me or support me like most parents would or should. This is when the rebellion and fights started. Unfortunately, they were not equipped to properly reprimand or communicate to me what I needed. If I objected or questioned something, they disapproved, and the most common response was, "Because we say so." This, of course, didn't sit well for long. I'm sure, at times, it was very difficult to deal with a rebellious teenager; especially one who was constantly being mocked and picked on because of who they were and how we lived.

I remember our church and my grandmother putting money up to send cleaning companies multiple times to our little apartment, to have it cleaned and fumigated. If I told you exactly how I lived as a child, you probably wouldn't even believe it. There was so much garbage, junk, and cat feces all over the floor all the time that nobody in their right mind should have lived under those horrid conditions, let alone raise a child there.

My teen years weren't much better. I dropped out of school in grade 9. Then, after leaving my parents and being homeless, my grand-mother quickly arranged to have me put into foster care.

I don't know if that was much better, but it did put me on a very different and darker path, meeting people I probably shouldn't have met, and getting in with the wrong crowd. By the time I was 18, I was heavily addicted to drugs and alcohol, and not doing much with my life.

At 18 years old, I was also too old to be in foster care, so I had to move out. I ended up getting a job stocking shelves at night in a grocery store, and I slept on the couch of a buddy of mine. For me, this was what life was like: no education, no vision, and no hope.

By now, you're probably starting to wonder what all of this has to do with finances and attracting wealth. The reason I tell you this is not for you to feel sorry for me, but so that you can imagine that my initial understanding and ideas about money during these early years of my life were not conducive to building any kind of wealth or security.

Growing up, my parents never taught me anything about money, saving, investing, or even how to open a simple checking account. Whenever my parents received any money, it was immediately spent. Pay the bills first, and then have fun with the rest. That was their motto. This was something I, of course, picked up unconsciously and copied myself for years, well into my mid-twenties. What I and my parents didn't realize, like the middle and lower class, was that there are defined laws to money—laws like gravity: it doesn't matter how old you are or where you come from; if you jump off a building, you're going to hit the pavement hard. Similarly, if you fight the laws of money, you will be broke and a slave to debt forever. If, however, you work with the laws, money will be your servant and will never be an issue for your entire life.

I remember overhearing conversations my parents had around money when I was young, and you've probably heard them, like *"money doesn't grow on trees,"* and *"you have to work too hard to make money,"* and *"the rich take advantage of people."* Being rich or wealthy was just a pipe dream to me. I honestly believed it was not achievable and was never going to happen.

Believe me when I say that no matter where you are in life, what age you are, how you were raised, your background, or religion, the only thing that matters is that at any moment you can make a choice and turn things around. You have the power within you to make yourself live the life that you truly want and deserve.

I still remember the turning point. I was 18, just being, and going nowhere in life, and then I got the call. It was my grandmother to tell me I had a new baby brother who had just been born the day previous. This was a bit of a surprise as I was an only child until then. It was even a surprise to everybody in my family, including my parents, as they had just separated a few months prior, and no one knew my mother was even pregnant. Being curious, I went down to meet my mother, whom I rarely spoke to.

When I walked up to see her, she had a healthy newborn baby boy in her arms. She passed the baby to me, and I sheepishly accepted to hold him. At that moment, I know something switched in my brain. I was looking at that baby, and I saw myself. I saw that baby's future, and if I did nothing, he would go through the exact same problems and hardships I went through, maybe even worse. It was at this moment that I decided to do a complete 180 degree turn in my life. I made it my goal to make sure that baby and my future children would never go through what I did.

My first action was to go back to high school immediately! I got another full-time job delivering pizzas. Even though people said I was crazy for going back to grade 9 at 18 years old, I ended up graduating on the honor roll and eventually got accepted into Humber College. After paying my own way through college, I wound up getting into sales. I became a sales manager and eventually worked my way up to be a director of operations for a solar energy company. That was only the beginning of my success. I now consider myself a financial architect, designing financial dreams one day at a time.

Looking back, it was because of that moment I can attribute all my current and future successes. I would not call myself super rich by any means, but I can now say that I no longer worry about my finances. This is something I now help people with when I work with clients; something I am truly grateful for daily.

WINKs and the next chapter

As you will notice, I have provided a page at the end of every chapter, with lines to help you on your journey. This is where you record **WINK**s. You're probably wondering what the heck are WINKs?? Well, it's just an acronym I thought of, which stands for "**W**hat **I N**ow **K**now." The concept is that most of these ideas relayed in this book can be thought of as secrets held by the wealthy or successful; so I am now relaying them to you, with a little wink of the eye, so you **Now Know**. Of course, one of the best ways to retain new information is to write it down. Feel free to write what you have learned, or any notes or ideas you might have. Be creative, have fun, and get excited for what's to come!

Exercise #1

Success requires action, so throughout this book, I have placed exercises for you to jump into. They don't have to be big actions, but if you can take regular, small, consistent steps, it will make a huge impact down the road.

Practising gratitude should be a daily occurrence. This exercise should take you no more than 5 to 10 minutes per day. Take out a piece of paper, or use the WINKs page at the end of the chapter. You can do this exercise when you wake up or just before you go to bed.

Write down a minimum of 6 items in your life now that you are grateful for. They don't even have to be big, monumental things. You could be grateful just for the sun coming up, or that you woke up this morning alive and well. When you sit and think, I'm sure there's a lot to be grateful for in your life. Writing these items down makes them stand out more in your mind.

An example might look like this: *I, Ryan Baily, am happy and grateful today for my two beautiful, healthy, and smart daughters, Eliana & Amelie.* Once you have your six items written out, take a quiet moment and close your eyes. With your eyes closed, say those items out loud and visualize them. Wait until you can clearly see them in detail and start to feel any kind of positive feelings. It may feel a little awkward at first, but trust me; after a few days, it will get easier, and you'll notice the benefits throughout your life.

Now, to get a better understanding of what I really want for this book, and the ideas outlined in it, continue reading on to Chapter 2. This is where I describe what I want for you, the reader, and what I hope you get from it.

W.I.N.Ks

_____

_____

_____

_____

_____

_____

_____

_____

_____

_____

_____

_____

_____

_____

Chapter 2
What's in It for You?

"Where there is no vision, there is no hope."
– George Washington Carver

When was the last time you really heard of a bank, public school, or government agency holding free financial education training? In my 34 years, I don't remember any.

The thing is, most people don't even think about why they're not wealthy. Most people just try to justify their financial situation by blaming it on the economy, the government, their upbringing, or their job. Not very often do people sit and take responsibility for their actions.

There was a book I read recently by Tony Robbins, *Money Master the Game*, which really resonated with me. At first, some of the concepts and ideas in that book seemed radical or off, but I was intrigued and wanted to know more. The book broke down issues within our current financial system, explaining that most people are getting gouged by excessive fees, taxes, and absurd conflict of interest sales that you can only just shake your head at.

Once I finished reading that book, I was so inspired and fired up about this new knowledge, I walked into 3 branches for the biggest banks in Canada. I politely asked their investment advisors questions that had been raised in the book, regarding both investments and fees. In an odd turn of events, I was politely turned away by all 3 branches. The managers stated that I knew enough, and I should just go invest elsewhere on my own. Really?? I knew enough just by reading a Tony Robbins book. No disrespect to Tony, as he's a great teacher and a man I look up to and admire, but if I know enough by just reading that book, then what are those nice-looking branch offices with their highly paid investment managers for anyway??

There's something sorely lacking in our financial system that is drastically affecting society, and it needs to change. I remember going to school to learn about English, math, and science. Never was the subject of budgeting, investing, debt management, or credit ever brought up. All the information that was given was in a transactional learning experience that was designed to have us all end up as happy, successful citizens. Is that the case, given the fact that only 2% of the population are currently classified as financially wealthy, or what some might call *rich*? When looking at your finances, do you feel happy or successful about it?

Maybe you are better off than most; in which case, congratulations and good for you. I have a feeling, though, that most of the people who read this book are on the opposite end of the spectrum and want change; and who knows, maybe, even if you are successful in your current career financially, you'd like to just learn a few new ideas, or gain inspiration that can take you to the next level. So, either way, get excited, as I am here to help you on that path!

You know, as much as social media has connected our population like no other tool in human history, it has also shone a light on and created another major issue.

One main issue is the hatred and negativity that can come from a portion of the population. Don't get me wrong; there is a lot of good out there, but a lot of people now use social media as an outlet to vent their anger, frustration, and callousness towards other people, which they wouldn't normally do, and in most instances, have never even met! It's almost daily that I read vicious posts on Facebook, Twitter, Instagram, and YouTube about how someone is "fat, ugly, or stupid" in addition to all the other derogatory posts that I'm not going to relay as I want to keep this book as family friendly as possible.

I know North America has been raised on the idea of freedom of speech, and I believe in this general idea. Fortunately, I was also raised with the idea from my grandmother that if you don't have anything good to say, then don't say anything at all. What most people fail to realize is how their small actions influence the greater society. This is something I wish all of us to help turn around.

Now I have a firm belief that, at their core, everyone truly wants to be happy, successful, and nice. It's their mental programming through a lifetime of bad rituals and beliefs that have led people to take such drastic, negative actions. In their mind, they believe, if they act out a certain way, it will produce results that will make them ultimately happier. Unfortunately, that is rarely the case.

"Where the focus goes, energy flows" is a motivational quote that I have heard from many success coaches and motivational leaders. People don't realize that by constantly spitting out all the negative thoughts they have in their mind, they are strengthening negativity in their lives.

My true intention is to create positive, lasting change in you, the reader. This way, you can go on to leave a lasting, positive change in the people, family, and friends in your life. If I make a lasting change in only 10 people with this book, those people can easily make a lasting change in 10 other lives, and that's 100 people right there! Then those people go and make lasting, positive change in 10 people in their lives, which pushes it up to 1000! The next level up is 10,000. So, you see, through compounding, it can easily become exponential. Trust me, in later chapters, I'll show you how to make those numbers into dollar values.

What I'm trying to point out is that yes, I want to help you organize your finances and attract more wealth, but to do that, you must prime your mind for success! No one in history with a negative outlook had wealth flow to them, and if it did, they typically lost it just as quick. There's story after story of lottery winners who won big, and then, a few years later, are broke, bankrupt, or worse off then they were before. My goal is to not only teach you how to make wealth but to set yourself up so that wealth will come to you with little or no physical effort on your part, and you'll be ready to maintain it.

Another goal I have for you, the reader, is to help you build lasting, strong relationships. It seems kind of odd in a personal finance book, I know, but I believe it's important. Without loving support from the people around you, the wealth will be short-lived and pointless.

There's an old saying that *"money doesn't buy happiness,"* and I'm a firm believer in this. There are tons of examples of successful celebrities and business moguls who have lost it all. They have millions of dollars, fancy cars, beautiful homes, and all the toys you can buy, but they resort to drugs, alcohol, or suicide. Robin Williams is a prime instance. The man created a great legacy for himself. He had millions of dollars, awards, acolytes and prestige. He had millions of fans and a beautiful family, all of whom loved and adored him. He, unfortunately, spent a lifetime battling addictions, until he eventually committed suicide. He made everyone happy except himself.

People don't want money. What they want are the feelings that they think money is going to give them. Money is a tool. It's what you do with it to make it grow and create wonderful lasting memories with the ones you love that matters most.

It's also very important to realize that wanting excess money isn't about greed either. When I was young, my parents instilled in me that wealthy people were mean and greedy. I can tell you I have met quite a few very wealthy individuals who are mean and greedy, but I have also met many more that were loving, caring, and wanted to give back. Likewise, I have met many mean and greedy poor and middle-class people, but also, I have met many loving and caring ones as well. Money doesn't make you; it only amplifies who you are inside. This means if you are generous and caring inside, money will amplify that, and you'll be more generous and caring. But if you're a real jerk inside, money will just make you a bigger jerk. The beauty is that you get to decide and choose how you want to live. Most people forget that fact.

One of the first things I always recommend to my clients when building wealth is to re-evaluate their social circle. Psychologists believe you are the sum of the 5 closest people around you, and this is something I can attest to. Unconsciously, you start to think and act like the people around you in order to fit in; that's human nature. After college, I hung around with people who I thought were friends but were only there to pull me down to their level. When I first started in sales, many of the people closest to me, including some family, encouraged me to stop selling and "find a real job." It wasn't until later that I realized they weren't trying to save me from failure but were just holding me to their level so they wouldn't look as bad.

One of the best directions I ever received from my first success coach was to clean up my social circle. As soon as I divorced some friends, my wealth started to take form. One way to think is that if you really want to become wealthy and change your life, start trying to socialize and mimic the people you want to be like. If you can't find any wealthy people to socialize with, read about them.

Now, another big opportunity to receive from this book and the concepts in it is the ability to drastically improve your lifestyle. As I mentioned a few pages ago, money doesn't buy happiness. This is true; what money does is buy freedom—freedom to do what you want, when you want, with whom you want.

It's obvious that in our current capitalistic society, money is a necessity. If you want your family to live longer healthier lives, you will need money to buy healthier food and medical support. If you want your children to have the best education, you will need money to pay for that as well. Pretty much every aspect of your life that you would like to improve or master will probably require some kind of capital to get there.

When reading and learning from the leaders of wealth and success from around the world, I have found that there are 3 areas of your life that must be in balance to your expectations of success and growth to enjoy a truly fulfilled life. Number one is your health. If you and your family are sick all the time, it will be very hard to be happy. Number two is your relationships. As we are social beings, we need a sense of connection to others. Number three is your finances to pay for it all.

The thing to note is that these three areas are symbiotic and feed off each other. If one area is misaligned and not to your expectations, it will affect the other two. Think about it. When was the last time you saw a super healthy, popular homeless person? It doesn't happen. Most people actively avoid going near one when walking down the street. Also, if you are constantly sick or ill, it makes it very hard to earn a decent income or make any new friends. Money, whether you like it or not, will affect your health and relations. Not too many people will want to be around you if you are constantly borrowing money from them.

By fixing this one aspect, and super charging this area of your life, it will have a butterfly effect to improve not only your lifestyle but the lifestyle of your spouse, children, grandchildren, great grandchildren, and potentially all the people you ever encounter. With that much at stake, don't you feel finances are something you should be paying more attention to?

Lastly, I want you to receive from this book the benefit of giving back. Everyone wants a truly fulfilled life. Through experience and study, I have found that the last piece of the puzzle to living to the fullest is educating and helping others.

Virtually every religion and spiritual concept has some sort of reason or purpose for life or existence. Pretty much everyone asks this kind of question at some point in their life: "Why am I here? What's this all for?" Research shows that people who either tithe, give to charity, or aid others in some way, live the happiest.

When I first heard this, I was kind of skeptical. I considered myself open minded, so I tried it anyway. At first, I gave to my church. Nothing happened at first, and I didn't feel any different. Then I started to donate junk around my house that I didn't really need anymore.

It wasn't until I saw and experienced this young girl pick up an old toy at a donation booth that it started to hit me. This girl was so happy that she received something that she couldn't afford, and it made me empowered to do more.

One of my future missions is to start a charity for underprivileged youth, remembering that the youth are our future. This is something I hope for you. Whatever gains or insights you get from this book, this is the most important one. Spread what you have learned, and help the less fortunate. You and I can make this world a better place, one person at a time.

Exercise #2

Now, for the next exercise, grab a separate piece of paper or use the WINK page at the end of the chapter. With this piece of paper in hand, try and write down any thoughts or ideas about how your parents or authorities (e.g., teachers or relatives) viewed money. It can be anything, like a sentence they said, or what you might have noticed on how they acted towards money. Once you've written down at least 20 points, compare that to your current view or habits with money, and your spending and saving habits. What you will typically notice is that some of these ideas will be parallel with yours.

I did this exercise with my wife 10 years ago, and the results were startling. My parents typically spent every penny after the bills were paid. A common phrase around my house was that you had to work very hard to get money. What do you think my finances were like? I, of course, picked that up. I used to spend every penny after the bills were paid, and I always tend to be a workaholic.

In my wife's case, she comes from South America, which on average has a lower income scale compared to North America. Most people in these countries must scrounge and save every penny, and are constantly worried someone might come along and rob them, due to higher crime rates. This is something she noticed in her and her family's money habits. Her father works hard but keeps most of his money in cash, being fearful of losing on investments. Her mother is a lovely woman but has a habit of trying to negotiate every sale for a lower price. I was once in a black-market area, and her mother spent 10 minutes negotiating a dollar discount on a $3 pack of batteries I was trying to buy.

My wife noticed these types of habits right away, as she tended to always spend time seeking out the best deals possible, and avoided taking any risk on investments out of fear of losing any capital.

Now, on to the **what**. Keep on reading to Chapter 3 to find out what you're going to need in order to achieve financial independence and live the life you truly want.

W.I.N.Ks

_____

_____

_____

_____

_____

_____

_____

_____

_____

_____

_____

_____

_____

_____

Chapter 3
Changing

"The starting point of all achievement is desire."
– Napoleon Hill

Have you ever sat and asked yourself, "Why don't I have what I want?" An unfortunate truth that happens in our society is that most people will not achieve their true potential. The main reason for this is because most people do not have the simple discipline to stop or start an action.

I am going to be very honest with you and tell you that if you want to be financially independent, you're going to have to develop some self-discipline. Whether you want to be physically fit, start a business, or want a long-lasting intimate relationship, you will have to develop self-discipline to get it, and financial independence is no different.

Think about it; if you really want to save for retirement, or buy that new Tesla Model S you've always wanted, you're going to have to be able to discipline yourself to not spend every penny you earn.

Unfortunately, self discipline has gotten a bad rap these days. Some people consider it to be a form of self-punishment—not doing what you want to do. The way I view it is more like self love or self sacrificing what you want right now in order to gain a greater long-term benefit. It's like saying, "I love myself too much and want to live longer, so I'm not going to eat that fatty cheeseburger," or, "I love myself too much to stay home studying when I could go out partying with friends."

I learned the hard way when I first started making six-figure earnings. I didn't make any silly mistakes such as bad investments or gambling debts. My issue was food and not controlling my expenses. When I first got into sales, I set targets for myself. If those targets were hit, I would treat myself to a nice dinner of lobster, steak, or something equally fancy—mainly because I figured I earned it. After a while, those innocent dinners of good intention added up to 2–3 thousand dollars per month. This put a very serious dent in my finances, and a strain on my marriage.

It's all fine and dandy to have the knowledge and support to make and earn a lot of money, but to be truly financially free requires you to control yourself and not indulge in every fancy thing you can think of. Warren Buffet, one of the best investors in history, has a saying that stands true. He states, "Don't save what is left after spending; spend what is left after saving."

Overall, there are two ways to really develop self-discipline. One way is by avoiding what you don't want. The second way is by focusing on what you do want.

At the beginning of my career, I focused on what I didn't want. I was terrified of the thought of my younger brother and my future children going through the same hardships I went through. This mindset only served me for a short while because, as I started making money, my drive dropped. It took me a while to figure out that I needed something more. I needed to focus on what I really wanted instead of what I didn't want. When I made that shift, changes really started to happen in my life.

Now, one of the biggest disciplines regarding finances is in being properly educated. The more you learn, the more you earn. I hear a lot of people saying that ignorance is bliss. Ignorance is not bliss; ignorance is pain and suffering, and a lifetime of financial hardships. Just look at the divorce rate in recent times. Almost 50% of marriages end in divorce now, and one of the top reasons is how the family finances are handled.

The rich get richer, and not because they take advantage of people or are mean or greedy. Don't get me wrong; there are people like that out there. The rich get richer because they know things that the middle class and poor don't. They educate themselves, and they surround themselves with other educated people, to learn as much as they can about money.

One side effect of starting a new path of being financially independent is that you may experience resistance. It seems odd, but humans tend to get jealous towards another person's success, even though nobody wants to admit it.

This was something I experienced firsthand. When I left the working world for commission pay, a lot of friends, and even a few family members, suggested I stop. They thought selling was low and what I was doing was not legitimate work. Initially, I took their negativity with a grain of salt and kept at it. It was a good thing I did this, however; the more money I made, the more aggressive some of them became. Over time, this aggression got so bad that these people either left my life or I had to avoid them altogether.

I once had a roommate who had just been laid off right around when I started in sales. Everything was fine at the start. He went on unemployment insurance. We had agreements in place for who would do the chores and how the bills were to be paid. One week I would clean; he would clean the next.

What ended up changing was my work schedule. After a few months, I started going on company business trips across the province for days at a time. When I returned, he would ask sarcastically, "How was your trip?" I was overly enthusiastic about what I did, so I told him how much money I made. At first, he baulked and shrugged it off, but after a while, he questioned all my responsibilities. I was fine to clean when I could, but I got so busy that I was never around and not making any of the mess. He didn't seem to care for that, and expressed his desire for me to do my share of the cleaning.

After a few aggressive arguments, I tried to compromise and pay for a house cleaner. I figured I didn't necessarily like cleaning, and I was making more than enough to pay for the cleaner. This ended up having the opposite effect of what I wanted. My roommate got even more upset that I would even consider a house cleaner. He asked who I thought I was, like it was some super lazy concept to have someone else do something I didn't want to do. My view was, if I don't like doing it, and it takes time, why not pay someone who enjoys doing that, so I don't have to? This way I can spend more time doing the things I enjoy, and use my resources to earn a higher income. Suffice to say, that friendship didn't last long, and we both went our separate ways soon after.

I did discover something useful out of that experience. Don't let people's opinions of you control your destiny. If you have a vision and a passion for something you enjoy doing, DO IT! Friends and family may try and dissuade you, but if you listen to the naysayers, it will drastically lower your income, and you'll never truly be free.

Easily, one of the greatest motivational speakers of the last 50 years must be Jim Rohn. I've watched many of his recorded seminars, which have helped me and countless others elevate themselves. Unfortunately, he had passed before I could attend one of his live seminars, but his message lives on.

One story that resonated with me was about the start of his career. He sat with his mentor and was told to set a ridiculously high goal of becoming a millionaire. Not only that, but he was to make sure that he really understood why it was good idea to become a millionaire. Mr. Rohn's reaction was bewilderment. He didn't understand why he needed to be informed about the reasons why it was good to become a millionaire. Most people think just having the money and freedom are enough reasons for wanting to become wealthy.

His mentor corrected him. He stated that it would be good for him to become a millionaire because of "the man he would become in order to achieve it." The idea was that to achieve such a goal would push and inspire him to new levels of skill, and that he would be a completely different person by the time he reached it. This is something that struck a cord with me and inspired me to be as great as I can.

A little note on learning new skills, which can be applied to wealth building. It's a common concept that there are four levels to learning any new skill. The first one is what is considered **unconscious incompetence**. What this means is that you don't know what you don't know. Take *Jeet Kune Do* for example. Most people don't know that this is a martial art created by the late Bruce Lee. Now, a moment ago, you probably didn't know that such an art existed, let alone how to perform it. Once you have become aware of a skill, you move from not knowing you didn't know about it, to the second level, which is **conscious incompetence**.

This is the level where you are consciously aware you don't know something; like how I'm consciously aware I don't know how to fly a helicopter. The concept I'm aware of, but my ability to perform it is still incompetent.

The third level of skill is **conscious competence**. At this level, you've begun to study and practice the skill but still must use a great deal of focus to perform it. A great example of this is when you first learned how to drive a car with a manual transmission. Do you remember the first few times learning to drive stick shift?

Hold the brake, turn off the e-brake, check your mirrors, push the clutch, put the gear in first, slowly release the clutch while now slowly applying gas, check your mirrors, push the clutch, put the gear in second, take your foot off the clutch, push the gas again, check your mirrors again, push the clutch, place the gear in third position, press the gas again, check mirrors, OH MY GOD, A RED LIGHT! Press the break, push the clutch, move the stick back to first position, stop the car, and phew... finally breathe.

I'm sure anyone can relate to the stress of this the first time they tried driving manual, but now what is it like? If you've been doing it long enough, a walk in the park, I bet.

That moves you to the final level of skill, which is **unconscious competence**. Hopefully, the level at which you drive a vehicle now. You are so proficient at the skill that you can do it with little or no active focus. It's at this level you start to use less brain power to do the skill, and you can concentrate on doing and learning additional tasks.

Now that you've stopped all your driving, don't forget the keys! Especially when one important key of success is consistency. Whether it's in your personal or business life, consistency is what keeps people trusting and believing in what you can do for them, and is the basis for your integrity. If you say you're going to do something, do it!

Imagine a marriage where the husband showed up sometimes to dinner without informing his wife. How happy do you feel that wife would be? In the office, do you think an office manager would put up with a staff member who handed in projects only some of the time? Time and time again, I see people who believe excuses are good enough for being inconsistent— my car broke down; traffic was bad; alarm didn't go off; my cat died—all excuses used so much you can almost feel which one is coming before it's said.

An old sales trainer of mine had a good saying when it came to excuses. "Excuses are like assholes: everyone has one, and they all stink." A little vulgar, I know, but true. I'm not denying that any of the previous events didn't happen; they probably did. If you allow excuses to take control of your life, you're lacking responsibility, and it's very hard to grow if you're not taking responsibility for what happens in your life.

Something I have always prided myself for is that if I say I'm going to do something, I will do whatever is needed to accomplish it. Like writing this book!

The big takeaway you should get from all this is that the rewards of building a secure financial foundation, and never worrying about money, vastly outweigh the struggles of getting there.

Over the course of this book, I will be asking you to do or try things that may feel a little uncomfortable, or that you may be fearful of. That's okay; do it anyway. If you don't feel uncomfortable, then there is no growth. It's like when you're body building. If you finish a workout and aren't tired or sore, you really didn't accomplish much. Your muscles grow when they're pushed and uncomfortable.

As for fear, being able to control that could be one of the best achievements you could ever accomplish in your life. Most people fear anything that comes with a risk of the unknown. You see, whatever you do in life is going to have some inherent risk involved—*everything*. Most people go get a *day job* to be safe, but is that really safe?

As I type this, a major General Motors factory in Oshawa, Ontario is shutting down after 100 years of operation, and laying off approximately 5,000 employees. Many of these men and women wanted a safe job with a safe pension, and some of them dedicated decades of their lives to get it. What do they really end up getting? A pink slip and a "have a good day, best of luck."

An analogy I like to use for success is skydiving. No matter where you're from, or what your background, religion, or income is, skydiving comes with an inherent level of risk.

Now, about 80% of the population is so afraid of skydiving that they won't even get on the plane, let alone jump out of it. Now, for the next 15%, they jump onboard and blindly go up and jump out without analysing things—Does the trainer know what he's doing? Did I pay attention during the training? Is my parachute packed properly???— only to SMACK, and hit the pavement hard.

It's the last 5% that take the risk, but they make sure it's a safer, calculated risk. They study and study during the training classes. They research their trainer to make sure they're qualified and have lots of experience in order to make their first jump with them. They check and double check their parachute. Then, finally, they pump themselves up and JUMP! It's this 5% that battles their fear through prep and being educated, which eventually leads them to becoming successful.

Even with all the prep work, though, there is still the possibility to hit the pavement. What makes these people even more special is that they get back up, dust themselves off, and go at it again until they do make it.

Now the question is, are you going to have what it takes to make a difference in your financial future?

Exercise #3

Take a piece of paper or use the WINKs page. Write down a brief paragraph or a few sentences of changes you'd like in your finances, and why you want them. It might be that you have debt and want to pay it off, or you might want to double your income. A little note is that you should write this always in the present positive point of view, as if it has already happened, with a date for a deadline. Don't worry about how you're going to get it; we'll get to that later. The most important thing is that you know what you want and why you want it. An example of this would be: *I, Ryan Baily, earn $500,000 per year by Dec 31, 2020. I achieved this, so I can fully support the lifestyle my family deserves while relieving stresses from my life.*

Now, to understand more about the money mindset and what changing your mindset can do for you, continue reading on to Chapter 4. This is where I describe the mindset you need in order to have a real impact on your finances, but also show some tips on how to change it.

W.I.N.Ks

_____

_____

_____

_____

_____

_____

_____

_____

_____

_____

_____

_____

_____

_____

Chapter 4
It's All in the Mind

"If you think you can or think you can't, either way you're right."
— Henry Ford

Did you know that there was a time when you could not walk across a room from one side to another? Do you remember when that was? Unless you had a major accident or a disability of some kind, you probably can't. Very few people can remember those early days when they were a tiny little baby, unable to walk or speak, completely dependant on their parents.

Walking is such a normal activity now, and you have no problem believing that you can walk from one room to another. How did you get that belief? The most obvious answer is that you saw your parents walking and felt that you could do the same. Initially, things didn't work out. You probably fell down a few times, but with constant motivation from your parents, you eventually succeeded.

What happened since then? How come that belief didn't continue with everything else, like finances and wealth? The most obvious answer again is that you modelled your parents and early teachers.

When working with clients, the first step I take to achieving financial independence is cultivating a mindset of wealth. More than likely, you have unconscious programs about money that were embedded in you at a very young age. These ideas, to this day, mold you and affect how your results end up.

If your parents were always stressed about money when you were young, then you will most likely be very conservative and not willing to take much risk. If your parent, on the other hand, were carefree with money, you may have an issue with spending. The only way to correct any kind of issue is to first confirm and admit there is one.

One sure way to prime your mindset for wealth is to get rid of ANTs. Now, I'm not talking about the annoying insects that build nests in your driveway. I'm talking about Automatic Negative Thoughts. We all have them, and unless you take more control of your thoughts, you will never be able to build wealth.

The average person thinks a lot. It is estimated that everyone has around 60–80 thousand thoughts per day! That's a lot of thinking. The unfortunate thing is that most of these thoughts are negative. After a lot of psychological research, it was found that the average human is typically frustrated or upset with past events, or excessively worrying over future events. This means the present is the least thought about.

You may have heard the usual optimistic phrase as viewing the glass half full as opposed as half empty. A good quote I recently heard made a lot more sense about this. *"The people who talk about the glass being half full, versus half empty, are missing the point. The glass can always be refilled."* This is true, as most people forget that out of every living creature on the planet, we are the only ones who have direct control over how we think and feel. It's up to you how you view and experience your world. The best way to change your thoughts is to start being more aware of them.

Now, you might ask, "How do I know a thought is negative?" The simplest way is to stop and analyze how it makes you feel. If there's a feeling of anger, hate, doubt, jealousy, anxiety, or anything that makes you feel down, that would be classified as negative.

To change that to something more positive, hands down, the best method is practising the act of gratitude. When I started paying attention and being grateful for all the good things I had in my life—my health, my family, and my country, among others—I noticed, almost immediately, fewer and fewer negative thoughts popping up. I am only human, so I still get them from time to time, but I can control them and squash them before they turn into something more.

Now, do you ever feel like you just don't have enough time or energy to accomplish the things you want or need daily? We all have the same amount of time, but it's what we focus on that determines our results. If you look at someone who is physically fit, that person doesn't have more time to exercise. They just made it a habit and a standard to exercise every day, and you can see it in their results.

After studying some of the top coaches and successful business people in the world, I found one thing in common. They pretty much all had positive morning rituals to boost them and aid their brain through the day. What I started to do is implement some of these rituals or habits into my own morning, and I noticed a dramatic increase in my overall energy and focus.

Firstly, I found that our bodies are made up of 60% water, and our brains are made up of 73% water. After sleeping for 6–8 hours, some of that water depletes, and we become dehydrated. So, first thing I do now when I wake up is drink 1–2 glasses of pure water to replenish myself.

The second activity I do is to quickly make my bed. Some of you might ask why making your bed in the morning is important. If you're familiar with military training, making the bed is a ritual that is standard. The reason for this is that psychologists find that you get a release of positive endorphins in your brain whenever you accomplish anything. Starting your day with a positive accomplishment is a feeling that can carry on with you for the remainder of the day.

The next movement I do is jump into the shower. I'll wash myself, and then, near the end, turn the water on cold for 3–5 minutes. I know some of you might dislike and cringe at the idea of this, and I'll admit it was the hardest habit to implement. There are numerous studies that find having a cold shower or being exposed to extreme cold has numerous positive effects on the body. It restarts your nervous system, improves breathing, and lowers bodily inflammation. Sports athletes take ice baths or cold showers right after intense activity to sooth sore muscles. I also found that men and women in Northern China jump in freezing cold water regularly, as they believe it extends life.

Finally, the next habits I do, once dressed, is to meditate for 5–10 minutes to clear my mind, journal in my note book about my goals and thoughts, and finally, read for 15 minutes, every day. Leaders are readers, and this is something highly encouraged if you want to have real change in your life. Warren Buffet states he reads everyday for hours to improve his craft of investing.

Lastly, a habit that doesn't need to be created but more like broken, is our dependency on that little piece of plastic and metal—the cell phone! One of the biggest adjustments I made was to commit to not looking at my phone for the first hour of the day. You notice that everyone now is glued to their phone, responding to texts, watching their social media, and responding to emails. All this activity is training our minds to be more reactive as opposed to proactive. As soon as you look at your phone, you're essentially reacting to the world. Keeping it off allows you to feel more like you are in control, and not the world around you. Commit to not looking at your phone for the first hour of the day. You can thank me later.

A man I know, who had lots of positive habits and visions, was a man named Roger Bannister. In 1954, Roger completed what everyone at the time thought was impossible. He was the first man to run a full mile in 4 minutes. Before this achievement, every doctor and scientist thought the ability to run that fast was virtually impossible. The thought prevailed that if you did run that fast, your heart would literally explode in your chest.

Roger didn't think that way. He practised over and over, and after he ran that distance, reporters asked how he was able to do it. His explanation was that during his training he would envision himself crossing the finish line at 3:58 seconds, over and over. Remember, *where focus goes, energy flows.*

What got him to accomplish this was a combination of positive daily habits, setting a high standard to practise, and a strong, clear vision. An interesting note is that once he had broken the record, about a dozen other individuals ended up beating the exact same record within the next few years. Now that he had done it, everyone else had belief. Just keep that in mind. Successful people believe it, and then they see it. Unsuccessful people see it, and then they believe it.

Exercise #4

Take a piece of paper or use the WINKs page. Write down at least 4 new habits you can do every morning to start your day off right. Once you have those written down, grab a few flash cards. Write one habit on each flash card, and tape those cards in areas that you know you will walk by in the morning, like on a door you'll have to open, or on the mirror in the washroom.

It's unfortunate, but most people are overly groggy and tired when they wake up, and completely forget about these new habits they were supposed to do. Having these flash cards around will remind you as you start your day. It will only take a few weeks, but if you keep at them, they will start to build into habits that you don't need to be reminded of. Take note of any positive changes you see or feel after implementing them.

To find out how to change and really dive into the meat and potatoes of financial education, continue reading on to Act 2 and Chapter 5. This is where we describe the universal tactics of having control of your finances and what you can start doing right away.

W.I.N.Ks

Act 2

How to Change???

Chapter 5
Life Within Means

"It isn't what you earn but how you spend it that fixes your class."
– Sinclair Lewis

To start off the second act, I want to congratulate you! You've made it this far. It's a sad statistic that 75% of people will never pick up a book after they finish their primary education of high school, college, or university. You are one of the few that acts as opposed to the many that just talk. Give yourself a pat on the back!

Now, down to the nitty gritty. Whenever I work with clients, I am shocked that most mature adults either don't know how or don't do any form of household budgeting. One of the biggest misconceptions is that making more money will solve your problems. Unfortunately, if you spend more than you make, and don't control your cash flow, you will never be financially independent.

You can read about celebrity upon celebrity who made millions, only to declare bankruptcy for bad money management. Kim Basinger was a superstar in the 80s, with film hit after film hit. She had to declare bankruptcy in 1993 due to a bad business deal. The singer, 50 Cent, and the singer, Meat Loaf, as well as actor, Burt Reynolds, among others, made millions and lost it all due to lack of control over their finances.

It's sad that until I got financially educated, I never did any form of budgeting either, but you need to. Most Americans and Canadians are living paycheck to paycheck, and an unexpected job loss or market downturn can be devastating.

A budget or a financial statement, in its simplest form, is just a piece paper or excel sheet that is a way of being intentional about the way you spend and save your money. All you do is write down all the expenses you have on a monthly basis. This would include your mortgage payment or rent, utilities, property tax, insurance, cable, cell phone, internet bills, groceries, home maintenance, and debt repayments. Once you have all these payments, take your gross monthly income, and deduct the income taxes and all your monthly expenses to get your remaining net income. So, income minus expenses—simple. If, after calculating, it's positive, that's good. If it's in the negative, then we have a little work to do.

What a budget really does is keep you focused on your goals. What naturally happens is that you start to avoid spending unnecessarily on items and services that do not contribute to attaining your financial dreams.

Even cutting out a daily latte, smoking, or any number of small daily habits can have the long-term effect of improving your wealth. A $3.00 Starbucks latte daily is roughly $90.00 per month saved. Invest and compound that conservatively at 6% in a tax deferred account over 30 years, and that is $90,505.81 extra for retirement! Where can you save?

If you look online or speak to a financial professional, they'll gladly give or create a simple budgeting tool for you to get started.

One of the bonuses that comes along with this book is a simple to use excel budgeting sheet that I use with my clients. Go to **www.moneymagnetpath.com** to download and get your free bonus. In time, the excel sheet will be updated to a smartphone app to make access and convenience easier than ever.

Now, regardless of whether your expenses are good or not, you should take the time to re-evaluate all your monthly expenses. If you really want the expenses you've got, and want higher means in life, then you need to start developing passive income streams to cover these, which I will get into in a later chapter.

Start with your major expenses first. Your mortgage or rent payment will most likely be the biggest. Rule of thumb in the industry is that your housing payment should be no more than 28% of your net income. I'd say 25% is a better option to make things safer. This means, if your total net income (after income tax deductions) between you and your spouse is $5,000 per month, your housing payment cannot exceed $1,250.00.

If you are breaking the 25% rule, then you need to shift something. Maybe speak with a mortgage broker to see if you can get a better rate or an extended plan. Maybe investigate renting out spaces in your home, like rooms or the basement. Even a garage can be rented individually as storage space. I've seen them rented for a few hundred per month. Heck, you might be able to even rent out your roof. There are a few solar energy programs that might be able to cover the cost of installation in exchange for energy produced.

The last option, which is usually the hardest, is maybe to look at downsizing. Ask yourself whether you really need the extra space you have. Do you really need what you have, or do you just want what you have? Making that distinction is very important to financial success.

Now it's time to evaluate your transportation. Do you need that Mercedes, or could you do with a Honda? Just by buying an older vehicle, 3–5 years old, you can save yourself some money, as a car drops 10% in value the moment you drive it off the lot. Remember to always factor mileage usage and insurance into your figures. Having a higher deductible on your auto insurance can save you a decent amount every year.

Once you've figured out your living expenses and transportation, move onto the other regular bills, such as utilities, cable, internet, insurance, and cell phones. Take a moment each month to re-evaluate your plans and usage. For utilities, check to make sure you have tuned up and high-efficiency heating and/or cooling equipment, high-efficiency light bulbs, appliances, windows, doors, and even toilets. They may be more expensive to install, but the energy savings will be well worth it in the long run. Have an energy audit done to see where you could save more. Having a smart thermostat installed and programmed alone can save you a few hundred dollars a year in wasted energy.

For the other bills, shop around regularly. There are plenty of internet resellers that can save you a bit, and cell phone companies are constantly giving out offers to attract more business in this competitive marketplace. Even sometimes calling up your current provider, saying you're thinking of switching, may entice your current company to offer a discount.

Now, the last of your regular expenses is probably the hardest to control: groceries! It's unfortunate we live in a heavily marketed society, and food is a huge part of that. A few ways to keep food expenses down is by having a list and budget prior to shopping. Unfortunately, when most people go without a list, they are primarily controlled by their unconscious needs and desires, which never really works well for your bank account. Having a list keeps you on track.

Another simple trick to keep your subconscious at bay is to eat right before grocery shopping. Studies find that people spend more when they are hungry, as their brain is giving signals constantly about that need. Eating prior shuts that signal down and allows you to think from a more logical standpoint.

The last note is to avoid taking children shopping with you. I know this is hard, as I have 2 young daughters and understand this too well. Most packaging is designed with children in mind, and marketing companies know this. Having your child with you only allows the child to plead and beg you to buy those cookies that you don't really want or need. There is nothing worse than your child making a scene and forcing you to buy them anyway.

A way to also control your expenses is to have multiple accounts open for specific expenses. An example would be to have one bank account only for house expenses, or maybe one credit card specifically for groceries. This makes it easier to track your money and know where it's going.

As I had mentioned earlier in Chapter 2, I read the book, *Money Master the Game,* by Tony Robbins. The underlying point of that book is to make sure you pay attention to small account fees and taxes, both of which can have a devastating effect on your retirement saving. Even a 1% fee can add up over time.

Take this hypothetical situation: two neighbours save $1,000 per year, for 30 years, in a tax deferred account. Now, let's assume neighbor one achieves a consistent interest rate of 10% per year—not bad. This neighbour would produce a final savings nest egg from compound interest of $176,735. As for neighbour two, he managed to get a consistent interest rate of 9% per year— only 1% difference. Now, you would think these two situations would end very similar, but neighbor two ends up with $148,575. Still a very decent haul; however, compared to neighbour one, he ends up with $28,160 less, or about 16% less for his savings. Keep in mind, this example is hypothetical, but it goes to show that a 1% difference in interest or fees can have a drastic effect on your retirement for the long run.

Be sure to read and know what fees you are paying for when it comes to accounts, mutual funds, mortgages, and investment advice. Whenever possible, get advice from a professional and know their fees as well.

As for tax, make sure you hire an accountant who works for you and completely maximizes your situation from the tax man. In North America, we pay some of the highest tax rates. To be wealthy, you need to be as tax efficient as possible. Overall, the average person pays close to 50% of their hard-earned money to the government.

Now, I don't have anything against the government, as I feel we live in one the safest and cleanest areas in the world, which is paid for by our taxes, but I don't want to pay more tax than I need to.

It is in your best interest to get an accountant that arranges it so you pay the least amount possible. I hear of some people who choose to do their taxes on their own or get a U-file tax software to save some money. I think this is a mistake; wealthy people pay top dollar to their accountants to make sure their calculations are done accurately, and that they maximize their deductions as much as possible. In the long run, a good accountant can save you way more than they will cost you. In your life, taxes will be the costliest expense, as we pay tax for pretty much everything.

Now, I do get, from time to time, clients asking about setting up a corporation. There are pros and cons to doing this for tax reasons. If you're a higher income bracket, or self-employed, it may make sense to set one up. Unfortunately, every situation is specific, and it's wisest to ask a corporate accountant in your region to look over your situation and advise when incorporating would be good for you. There are extra fees and costs involved for setting one up.

One thing is for sure: one of your primary financial goals should be to get out of debt as quickly as possible. Debt, such as credit cards and lines of credit, have become a way of life.

In 2018, the average American has a credit card balance of $6,375, up almost 3% from last year, according to an annual study on the state of credit and debt in America. Total credit card debt has touched its highest point ever, surpassing $1 trillion. More than half of people also now think it's acceptable to default on their mortgage if they can't afford it.

Canadians are doing even worse, as the average debt load is now up to $22,081, a 3.6% rise since 2016. The average Canadian now owes

$22,081 in consumer debt, a figure that doesn't take into account any mortgages.

A common question among families is whether to start saving for retirement or paying off debt. In my professional opinion, and others, it's both! When paying off your debt, there still seems to be a bit of confusion on which debts to pay off first. Rule of thumb is a roll up structure. What this means is to make a list of all your debtors, and arrange them from lowest interest rate to highest.

Example: Creditor	Balance	Interest Rate	Monthly payment
Mortgage	$325,000	2.8%	$1,925.00
Car loan	$10,000	7%	$225.00
Line of credit	$15,000	8.5%	$175.00
Credit card 1	$5,000	19%	$100.00
Credit card 2	$3,000	21%	$60.00
Store credit card	$1,000	48%	$10.00

Now, the most efficient option would be to see if a mortgage refinancing would be possible to rollup all the lower debt into one payment at 2.8% interest. The biggest thing to remember for this is that you must be disciplined and not rack up debt again. All the monthly payments that were normally going to the debtors must now go towards your mortgage to pay it down even faster. Unfortunately, this tactic is dependant on your current mortgage rules and how far along you are in your term. Speak to a broker to find out, as sometimes the fees involved might or might not be worth it.

The next option is to always pay the minimum payment, and any extra money you have budgeted to your debt repayments, put towards the highest interest rate debtor. In this scenario, it would be the store credit card at 48%. Once this card is paid off, all funds budgeted can move to the next highest interest rate, which would be credit card 2, and so on.

This is where the self-discipline comes into action. It's imperative, once you have paid off a debtor, to either hide or destroy the cards. Either way, you must prevent yourself from using it, or else you will be stuck in the viscous debt rat race. A side note: Do NOT cancel a paid off credit card. You might think it will be better to close the account, but this will have a negative impact on your credit rating, and of course you should be checking your credit report once a year anyway.

Keeping an eye on your credit report helps against fraudulent activity, and lets you know how money lenders are likely to react to you. Not all credit is bad; you just need to know how to use it.

Now, let's say you're in insolvent territory, or are unable to keep up with your debts—another method must be used. Avoid going the route of bankruptcy or consolidation companies, as these methods will also negatively affect your credit and don't build your responsibility.

Take your list of creditors. One by one, list the debts by the age they were created. Once you have this list, contact each creditor and inform them that you will be paying off each creditor, but that you will be paying off the oldest debts first, and put all your budgeted debt repayment to that one debtor. Once a lender is paid off, you move to the next. Let each creditor know what position they are in and how much you will be paying.

This method is the most responsible way to deal with your debts. You put yourself in this position, so you need to own up and make good. Obviously, some creditors may whine and complain, but this will put you on the right moral track of keeping your debts at bay.

Physiologically, it makes you more responsible for your actions, as most people try to hide from collectors and people for whom they owe money. The first step in solving a problem is owning up and taking the heat. This will probably be extremely difficult at first, but you will be far better off once you've succeeded.

Another important aspect to understand in your day-to-day life is being able to tell the difference between an asset and a liability. Rich people buy assets, and the middle and lower class buy liabilities they think are assets.

Robert Kiyosaki, in his best-selling book, *Rich Dad, Poor Dad*, broke down the definition of assets versus liabilities in very simple terms. The simple definition of an asset is something that puts money in your pocket; whereas a liability is something that takes money out, so you need to control your cash flow.

One common myth is that your car is an asset, and most banks will try and use it as such. When you stop and think about it, a car does nothing but take money out of your pocket. If you purchase it brand new, it loses roughly 10% of its value the moment you take it off the lot. Once you own it, it will continue to lose value, and you'll continue to put out money for gas, insurance, and regular upkeep. This will go on for approximately 7 years until the car dies or is worn, and you go out to get another one and do it all over again.

Probably the biggest debate for an asset is your home. Most people will tell you it's an asset, and it can be, but it depends how you use it. Yes, the home should increase in value over the time you own it, but you still pay out for bills that never end. Mortgage, property tax, electric, gas, water, and maintenance are all costs that will come out of your pocket. Now, if the rise in value can cover all these costs for all eternity, then yes, it would be an asset. This, however, is highly unlikely.

The best way to turn your home into an asset is to generate income to cover some of these costs. Ways to do this is to rent out rooms or your basement. This really goes for any real estate investment. The income received must cover all the required expenses to be truly classified as an asset.

I made a bad call earlier in my career to buy a house with a friend from college and rent out extra rooms. Initially, it was a good idea. We were nice and rented them out to a friend and my girlfriend, who got large discounts on the monthly rent. After a few years, my accountant reviewed my statements, and we had been losing money almost from the start on this so-called investment property. I eventually sold that property, but it was a good learning experience to be more educated, because lack thereof can be costly.

So, don't waste time and energy buying liabilities. Learn to buy assets. As soon as you become an owner/investor instead of a consumer, you'll be right on your way to endless wealth.

Exercise #5

Do a budget! Go to **www.moneymagnetpath.com**, and download the free pdf or excel spreadsheet to calculate your monthly expenses. To be effective, a budget should be done monthly. Once completed, start and look where you can reduce expenses. Re-evaluate your costs, and shop for cheaper providers. Personally, I write my expenses on the printed version of the pdf and then transfer those numbers to the excel sheet to save. Writing things down makes them stick better in your mind and keeps you on track.

Now, to find out how to take control of your income, and improve your cash flow, continue reading on to Chapter 6. This is where I lay out the foundation to your financial dream house.

W.I.N.Ks

_____

_____

_____

_____

_____

_____

_____

_____

_____

_____

_____

_____

_____

_____

Chapter 6
Save and Invest, Duh?

"Tell me, and I'll forget. Show me, and I may not remember. Involve me, and I'll understand."
– North American Indian Proverb

Have you ever heard of the stereotype that Jewish people are wealthy? I'm pretty sure you have. Every time I run workshops for finance, *being Jewish* is a common term brought up from someone in the audience when the topic about savings comes up. Unfortunately, it's not completely true, as I have met a few Jewish people who were not wealthy, but I understand the idea.

Through my search of financial knowledge, one question I asked myself was how the Jewish people got this brand, and how did some of them actually obtain this generational knowledge of wealth? I eventually ran across a book, *The Richest Man in Babylon*. Written by George S. Clason, it was the account of an archeologist who was tasked with translating ancient tablets of the Babylonians in the early 1900s.

When ancient Babylon was unearthed in modern day Iraq, a library of tablets were discovered, which were thought to be stories of war and pillage. This was far from it; these tablets contained 3000-year-old stories of financial literacy.

Told from the perspective of a poor chariot maker, Bansir, it recounted his training and eventual rearing to financial independence. The Babylonian cultural was known through ancient history to be one of the strongest financially, and not through force or luck, but through business, trade, and sound financial habits. Where it gets interesting is that in 605 BC, it was known that King Nebuchadnezzar II of Babylon did invade Judah, which was home to the Israelites at the time, as depicted in the Bible's Old Testament. In the chapter of Daniel, it recounted that Daniel and a few other Israelites were summoned to the king after the Israelites' defeat. The king demanded the Israelites learn the Babylonian culture and literature. The men eventually agreed, and now, after 2,500 years, these ideas hold strong and true, and are the basis for pretty much every great financial playbook.

By far, the most important first rule given was the initial rule to *pay yourself first!* This rule is simple but something people fail to do. Most people who have a *job* will typically get their cheque and pay the government first through taxes. Next, they take what money is left and pay their bills. Then they will have some form of entertainment as well, which costs more money. Lastly, if there is anything remaining, they might put it in some form of low interest savings.

If you want to be financially free, you will need to learn to pay yourself first! You work hard for your money. Do you really want that hard-earned money to go to someone else, before you?

The golden rule is to always save a minimum of 10% of your income before anything else. I know it might sound hard if you've never done it, so if 10% is not an option, start with 2% or 3%. Start with whatever you can, and build up towards 10%. If you start low, after a few months, move to 5%, and then to 7%, and so on. The idea is to make saving habitual; this way, you will have money to invest for your future.

The way I now view saving is that every dollar I save is like having a tiny little financial soldier. That soldier can go out every night and day to work hard to make more money; and that way, I don't have to. The good thing about a money soldier is that they don't get sick, they don't get tired, and they don't complain. That's the best kind of soldier.

Now, I know you might be asking, "I have a job, and my taxes are deducted; how can I save first?" Simple: set up an automated retirement savings plan or pension through your employer, or have a tax deferred savings account, like a 401K in the U.S., or an RRSP in

Canada. This way, at least the savings is coming from pre-tax income and can usually be deducted directly from your paycheque.

I once knew a woman who was in serious trouble financially, and was close to bankruptcy. I had mentioned the concept of paying yourself first, and of course, she was totally opposed. Her rationale was that her debts were surmounting and she could not keep up with the minimum payments.

After a short conversation, we restructured her finances and set up a savings plan of .05% of her monthly income. Now, at this point, she was only working part time; so that .05% only equated to around $5 per month. You are probably wondering what $5 a month could possibly do for anyone, especially someone who was in debt. She was committed though, and decided to increase the money she saved every few months. Now, after two years of doing this, she is now saving around $7000 per year, and she has reduced her debt to half, while avoiding bankruptcy— not bad, eh?

Once a savings plan is put into place, and debts are going down, the next thing you must do is set up an emergency fund. Murphy's Law states, "Anything that can go wrong, will go wrong." That's part of life. Cars break down, basements flood, and accidents happen.

If you have an emergency fund put aside for a rainy day, you won't have to rely on going back into debt. To be safe, an emergency should be 3–6 months of your household expenses. So, if your monthly expenses were $4,000.00 per month, you would need to put aside between $12,000 and $24,000.

I recently had my own medical emergency a few months prior to completing this book. I had just quit my cushy corporate job to go on as a freelance financial advisor. Perfect health, a fiery attitude, and not a care in the world—until it hit me.

At first, the symptoms I had were very similar to the flu. The first two days, I brushed it off and told myself I was fine; all I needed was rest. This wasn't the case. By day three, I started to get a splitting pain in my abdomen, which made it very difficult to even walk.

Unfortunately, my wife had just left to South America a few days prior with the kids to visit family, so I was home alone. Scared and in pain, I called an ambulance. I was taken to the hospital and had an x-ray, and I found out immediately that my appendix had ruptured inside me. I was rushed immediately into surgery and spent four days in the hospital.

Talk about hitting the pavement! A few days prior, I was so fired up about my new life I left a secure paying corporate job to go solo. What happens next?? I'm bedridden and alone for a month. The surgery was a success, but it took longer than normal for me to heal, with heavy medication to boot. I couldn't write or deal with clients.

Luckily, a few months prior to this, my wife and I had setup an emergency fund. Because of this, I could focus on healing and not stress about how the bills were going to be paid, and avoid going into debt. That period taught me to be more grateful for every day, as you never know what may happen next.

One of the best quotes I've ever heard is, *"Yesterday's the past, tomorrow's the future, but today's a gift. That's why it's called the present."* So, save yourself and your family tons of stress and aggravation in the future by setting up an emergency fund. When an emergency strikes, you'll be prepared!

Now, the best way to protect you and your savings from a potential downfall, or problems beyond your control, is to **diversify!** I am sure you have heard the old saying, *"Don't put all your eggs in one basket."* The most common place this term is used is when investing in the stock market and buying various stocks in various industries, to protect yourself from losing all your capital; although it can be referenced to any financial act of spreading out your money to reduce losses.

The concept is simple, but when you place your money in only one type of asset—let's say real estate, for example—you then, by definition, are exposed to all the risk that could potentially happen within that real estate market. In the event you had money in the U.S. real estate market during the 2008–2009 market crash, you would have more than likely lost most, if not all, of your investment at that time.

Being invested in multiple asset classes protects for the long run like holding various stocks, bonds, and real estate at the same time. Not only saving and investing in different classes, but also investing in different geographical areas and at different times is another way of diversification. What happens in one geographical area is typically not happening in a different area at the same time.

If the S & P 500 index goes down, which is just a collection of the top 500 U.S. publicly traded companies, then other markets in Europe or Asia may or may not be affected, and could even go up.

Now, there is debate regarding what and how to invest in order to have enough diversification. I'm not going to say there's a one-fits-all type of solution. What really matters is your personal financial goals and how far along you are in your path.

I'm licenced with an investment brokerage that specializes in free financial education. If you are interested in getting an opinion, or even a second look if you already have an advisor, on your own financial plan, feel free to email RBaily10NENC@wfgmail.ca. The advice given out is free, confidential, and a no-obligation second opinion.

Probably one of the most important discoveries in financial history was the discovery by Albert Einstein, *the rule 72*. With this rule, it shows a simple formula to calculate the long-term effect of compound interest on a given investment. Take the number 72 and divide it by the % rate of return to give you the amount of years it takes for an investment to double in value.

Example of the rule 72 at work:

72/4 = 18		72/8 = 9		72/12= 6	
Money doubles every 18 years		Money doubles every 9 years		Money doubles every 6 years	
Age	4%	Age	8%	Age	12%
29	$10,000	29	$10,000	29	$10,000
		38	$20,000	35	$20,000
47	$20,000	47	$40,000	41	$40,000
		56	$80,000	47	$80,000
65	$40,000	65	$160,000	53	$160,000
				59	$320,000
				65	$640,000

*The rule of 72 is a mathematical concept that approximates the amount of years it will take the principal to double at a consistent rate of return. The performance of investments varies over time and, as a result, the actual time it will take for an investment to double in value cannot be predicted with certainty. This is a hypothetical example and is not intended to represent a real investment. Both the principal and returns of investments will vary over time. Seeking higher rate of returns involves higher risk.

Looking at these 3 scenarios, they all started with the initial $10,000 investment at the age of 29 and kept it growing until retirement at age 65. The difference between a 4% rate of return and a 12% rate of return, over 36 years, is $600,000! Which would you rather have?

It's a sad fact that most people are stuck giving their money to banks and accepting a lower rate of return. When you dig deep down and think about it, how do the banks make money? They invest it! They take your hard-earned money, offer you a lousy 0–2% interest in a guaranteed investment or savings account, and then lend it out to other people, like you, through mortgages, lines of credit, and credit cards.

The way to be truly financially suave is learning how to trade places with the bank. Borrow money at a low interest rate, and invest at a higher rate of return. This is what is called **Leveraging**. Now, as I said before, not all debt is bad. Used wisely, it can be a useful tool.

The thing with compounding is that it can make you or break you. If you have bad debt, it will compound your problem. Therefore, people who are constantly using credit get stuck in a rat race that never seems to end. They are paying higher interest charges and get frustrated when it seems as if their debt is not going down. On the other hand, if you're investing and taking advantage of compound interest, it will make you and your children, and your children's children, wealthy beyond imagination.

A lot of poor people just lack the knowledge to break free of the new age slavery, which is debt. Some know and don't do anything about it, or don't care enough to understand, but knowing is only a small part of the battle. It's disciplined action and patience that will lead you to success.

Einstein himself was quoted as saying, *"There is no force in the universe more powerful than compound interest."* Knowing this fact alone can have such a dramatic effect of your wealth and life in your retirement years.

Exercise #6

Make an appointment with a financial advisor or planner. Go online and look up 2 to 3 in your area. It's best to get a face-to-face meeting to get a real feel for the person you may be placing your entire financial future on. Most will do an initial meeting for free to look at your current situation. Make sure their fees, if any, are clearly disclosed. Some don't charge any initial fees but are compensated through providers who they recommend. Some charge fees upfront, or a percentage of annual investment earnings, ranging from 1–3%. As I mentioned earlier, I'm licenced with an investment brokerage that specializes in free financial education. If you are interested in getting a free opinion, email RBaily10nenc@wfgmail.ca. The advice given out is free, confidential, and with no obligation.

Now, to find out how to supercharge your income and find new ways to have your money make more money, continue reading on to Chapter 7. This is where we bring up a few techniques to invest like a champion and have your money make more money.

W.I.N.Ks

_____

_____

_____

_____

_____

_____

_____

_____

_____

_____

_____

_____

_____

_____

_____

_____

Chapter 7
MSIs for Anyone?

"There are no limits to what you can accomplish, except the limits you place on your own thinking."
– Brian Tracy

Now, money doesn't grow on trees. I think you know that. You must work for it or have some way to produce it. If you want to build wealth, there is a simple formula to know.

WEALTH FORMULA
INCOME
+ TIME INVESTED
+/- RATE OF RETURN
- INFLATION (Cost of Living)
<u>- TAXES</u>
= WEALTH

*This is a concept developed for illustration purposes only. The term "wealth" is subjective and must be defined on an individual basis.

Take whatever income you receive, add the time, add or subtract the rate of return on your investments, minus inflation and taxes, and this equals your wealth. Unfortunately, inflation and taxes are 2 things most people forget or neglect when looking at their finances.

Inflation is essentially your purchasing power. As a country prints more money, the value of said currency lowers. Therefore, investing is an important aspect of wealth creation, as slowly over time everything will cost more, which means you will be able to buy less with the same amount of money.

MSIs are the biggest secret held by the super wealthy. What the acronym stands for is ***Multiple Streams of Income***. There are two ways to generate income. Most people are raised on the first way of being *active*: they go to school, get good grades, get into a good college, land a good job, buy a house, build a family, and live happily ever after.

The reality is far from the truth. The idea learned from the ultra successful over the years is that having only a J. O. B. really stands for *Just Over Broke.*

Most students get into massive debt when paying for their education. Typically, their parents can only help them a bit with minimal savings. Once they graduate, they get a decent job, usually not what they studied.

From there, they meet the man or woman of their dreams; they get married and have a fabulously expensive wedding! Once they've tied the knot and the honeymoon is over, they buy a house and finance it with a 25-year mortgage. A couple years down the road, a baby pops out! This curbs their savings even more. They rack up more debt for all the junk to fill the house.

So, what do they do? They refinance their house and add all that debt back on the house. This cycle continues and continues until the couple hits retirement age, and they have next to no savings. They want to retire but only have a minimal amount in a savings or retirement account.

What to do? Only thing they can: sell their home, downsize, and pray to God the sum they receive lasts them till the end of their days. This repeats with their children, and the circle of middle-class poverty is complete.

The reason this scenario doesn't work is because most people are relying only on one asset: themselves and their ability to physically work! Now, I have nothing against work, but if you go to work, it should be for something you love, and only because you want to, not because you must.

The wealthy use their money to do the second option of making money, which is *passively*. They seek ways to buy assets that can appreciate or bring in regular positive cash flow to replace the income of a day job.

Diversification is an important aspect of investing, and it holds true with MSIs. This way, if one of your income sources were to go under, or stop all together, either by a job loss, government, or economic conditions, you still have income coming in from other sources.

Examples of MSIs can be stocks, bonds, income producing real estate, royalties from intellectual properties you produce or own, such as films, TV shows, music, or books, owning positive cash flow businesses, network marketing companies, ATM machines, and even social media outlets, to name a few.

Probably the most thought of and arguably the best way to invest is in stock and bonds. Essentially, the stock market is where shares of publicly traded companies are bought and sold. When you buy shares of a company, you are literally a part owner of said corporation. With that, you take on and share all the potential future profit and earnings of the company but also its downtime and losses.

A bond is another type of investment. It is a debt given out from a company, city, province, or even a country. If a corporation or municipality is trying to raise money but does not want to give up any equity ownership, it will usually offer bonds for sale, and the purchasers receive interest payments for the investment. Bonds are always issued a rating that indicates its credit quality. Private independent rating services provide evaluations of a bond issuer's financial strength or its ability to pay back the principle and interest in a timely manner. The lower the grade, the higher chance of default, but higher potential for earnings.

A common idea among investors is an idea called **Portfolio Theory**. In this theory, it brings up the idea that the greater the risk of a given investment, the greater the potential for earnings. There are plenty of debates on this theory; however, the stock and bond markets do come with their fair share of risk. A simple rule to live by when investing in markets is to only invest in what you know and understand.

Recently, a lot of chatter has been going on about Bitcoin being the latest and greatest investment; so much so that people are now putting their life savings into various Bitcoin companies. I just remember what Mr. Buffet said: *"Be fearful when people are greedy, and be greedy when people are fearful."* Since I also don't know much about Bitcoin, I personally would not be investing at this moment.

Coke is something I do know and understand, as I used to be in the food industry. Even though I try to actively avoid drinking coke, as there is zero nutritional value, I know people would rather buy a coke than a bottle of water. When I go to the grocery story, I see entire aisles of Coke products, and small sections for other healthier options. This is something that investors refer to as a blue-chip stock: a company that is consistently paying its investors with a wide demand and opportunity for growth—all the stats long-term investors love.

Now, you're probably wondering how one would navigate and know enough about every company out there to make an educated judgement about what companies to invest in. Well, to start, I don't care what anyone says. No one can predict the future. Anyone who says they only pick the best winners is straight up lying to your face. History has shown that no can correctly pick winning companies 100% of the time, and those who try to beat the market usually don't last that long.

In comes the **Mutual Fund**, a product designed to help the average Joe, like you and me. The first mutual fund was issued in 1924, and it allowed investors to invest in funds that held shares from multiple companies, which made it easier to diversify. The concept was sound; however, mutual funds come with their own problems and risk.

To start, mutual funds are now reliant on fund managers to pick and choose stocks, how much, and when to purchase. Some might argue that an active manager is a good thing, but as I had mentioned earlier, it doesn't matter how good you are at math, economics, or how many degrees you hold; no one can predict the future—no one. Some might do better than others, but history is not in their favor.

Second is the fees, as I had mentioned earlier in the book, reading Tony Robbins, *Money Master the Game*. This is what that book, and his follow-up book, *Unshakable,* centered on. What some people don't realize is that these funds are held by corporations that are first and foremost out to make a profit, and have attached fees, which are categorized in what's called a MER, or **Management Expense Ratio**. These fees can range from 2% up to 4% of your annual investment in the fund. Remember what the difference of only 1% can do to your retirement? Initially, you might say, "What's 2 or 4% between chums; these people need to eat." I get the idea of getting paid for service, but with understanding what that service is. Trying to read all the small print and get an outline of what fees are being charged is a nightmare, and most people are not going to spend a weekend doing it.

The other option, which is somewhat newer, is the ETF, or **Exchange Traded Fund**. These are funds that match a given index, like the S & P 500 in the U.S., or the TSX (Toronto Stock Exchange). Since you cannot actively invest in any index, these funds are set up to mirror them, so you take the good and the bad of the given market, keeping in mind that long-term growth is there. The benefit is that there is no active management, so these funds will have drastically lower fees of .03–2%. This, in the long run, can make a huge difference.

The takeaway here is that there is good and bad to investing in markets, and you should know your own risk tolerance. Remember that you should also know and understand what you are investing in, and seek the advice of a professional to make sure the investment is in your best interest.

On the topic of stock investing, a sad statistic is that 46% of the American population, and 65% of Canadians, mostly millennials, do not own any stocks or have any form of long-term savings plan from a 2017 study. When speaking with clients, the primary factor that most do not actively invest in the stock market or other asset classes is primarily out of fear.

The 2008 and dot.com market crashes are all too fresh in people's minds, and for good reason. These drops pretty much affected everyone in some way. Billions of dollars of wealth and retirement savings obliterated over night. A lot of uneducated individuals put their life savings into investments that they thought were good; however, these people did not truly understand what they were buying into. Most only bought as a get-rich-quick idea that they felt they should capitalize on.

The first thing to understand is that fear is a normal human reaction. We have a million-year-old evolved brain that is really designed to keep us safe and survive. Let me repeat that: your brain is there to help you survive, not thrive.

The problem stems from our evolution as a species. Back in the early days of man, you would run around hunting for food. On occasion, you might run into dangers, such as a sabre-toothed tiger. Now, over time, when it came to danger, through trial and error, humans began to rely on 3 basic functions to survive. These are commonly referred to as the freeze, flight, and fight mechanisms. When dangers arose, humans either instantly ran for safety, froze on the spot so not to be detected, or became overly aggressive in order to fight back.

Scientists have found through brain scans that we still use these mechanisms today, and a portion of the logical area of the brain shuts down, which leads to automated responses.

The problem now is that there is no sabre-tooth tiger, and we respond to other negative stimulus the same way. Brain scans have also shown that the loss, or even the potential loss, of money affects the mind the exact same way pain does. So, the loss of money affects us the same as being punched or stabbed. Now you can understand why some people avoid the stock market or investing, like the plague.

If you can get away from the emotional frame of mind (I know it's hard) and move to an educated logical stance, you will be much better off. Looking at historical data of stock markets shows some startling evidence. Take the S&P 500 again. In the last 100 years, there has been 13 major crushing drops to the U.S. stock market. Overall, most of these drops ended up being followed by some of the biggest gain bull markets in investing history.

The simple terminology used to describe a market is if a market drops more than 10% in value, it is referred to as a correction. If it drops more than 20%, it's called a bear market, and trust me, if you lose 20% of your investment in a short span, you feel like you've been mauled by a bear. The optimistic view of a market, where everything is going up, everyone is making money, and clear skies are ahead, is called a bull market.

A way to view it is like the seasons. Just as we go through winter, spring, summer, and fall every year, the stock market goes through ups and downs, but the long term is always up. Below is a graph of the S&P 500 over the last 30 years.

Market Summary > S&P 500 Index
INDEXSP: .INX

2,599.95 –50.59 (1.91%) ↓
Dec. 14, 4:59 p.m. EST · Disclaimer

| 1 day | 5 days | 1 month | 6 months | YTD | 1 year | 5 years | Max |

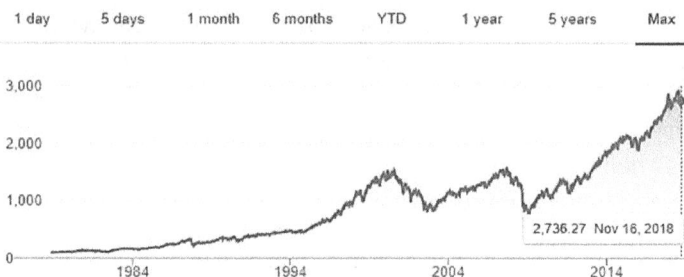

2,736.27 Nov 16, 2018

1984   1994   2004   2014

*Taken from https://www.google.com search results S&P 500 30-year historical data.

The takeaway is that investing is a long-term game. Sure, you might get a hit, but the stock market always rebounds. The math and studies show that you are far worse being out of the market than being in it because you must beat inflation as your money loses its value. The worse thing to do is to get emotional in a downturn and selloff, which unfortunately is what most people do.

Successful investors are always in the market and revel these moments. The primary reason is that when the stock market does drop, all the companies that are consistently successful are now being sold at discount prices. How would you feel about walking into a Ferrari dealership and finding out you could buy it for a quarter of the price?

The next asset class that has the potential to make massive earnings is in residential or commercial **Real Estate**. Probably the most underappreciated form of investing is the ability to buy a property and sell it to make gains and generate above average cash flow.

A mistake I made earlier in my career involved a troublesome property I bought with a roommate of mine after college. The reason I did this was when, in college, I noticed one of my primary expenses was my rent. I hated paying it, so my roommate and I, at the time, figured we could combine our savings to put down on a small property. It took a bit of time and pulling some strings, but we were able to get a mortgage on the property. Even after all the headache I went though with this first property, I was still able to turn a profit of $40,000 after all expenses.

Being a newbie, this was something that I couldn't ignore, so I started taking multiple real estate investment courses.

With real estate, there are 4 primary ways to make money. The first is the standard **house flip**. This idea is common, to buy a house that is either under valued or in need of renovations. Purchase the home, complete any lower-cost upgrades, and then sell the home as soon as possible for a higher price that will cover all costs, with a built-in profit. A simple example is below.

HOUSE EXAMPLE
Purchase Price - $500,000
Closing costs   - $20,000
Renovations   - $40,000
Carrying costs - $10,000
Total expense   = $570,000
Selling price   - $690,000
Realtor fee 5% - $34,500
Profit   = $85,500

*This example is for illustration purposes only. This situation does not represent an actual real estate deal as costs will vary. These will reflect the final gains, and this example does not take into consideration capital gains or land transfer taxes, which could vary by region.

The home is purchased for half a million, which if research is done, is lower than comparable properties in the area. Then subtract all closing costs such as lawyer fees, appraisal fees, and land transfer taxes. Subtract the renovations, which could be new appliances, flooring, or curb appeal. Subtract carrying costs for how long you own the property (3–4 months maximum), since bills like gas, hydro, property tax, and a potential mortgage still need to be paid.

Once that is all done, you pay a realtor top dollar to sell the property as high and as quick as possible to earn their commission. I know some people might try and save money by not using a realtor, but I advise against that. Unless you're already a realtor, let the professional do what the professional does. You're an investor, and the realtor's expertise will be valuable for doing what you want—selling high and fast! In the end, the profit was $85,500 on this deal for only a few months' time and little effort.

Now, if you think you need money to get into real estate, think again. The next strategy has made hundreds of millions able to buy and sell properties without investing a dime of their own money, *Real Estate Wholesaling*!

Real estate wholesaling happens when a person (the wholesaler) finds an undervalued home and puts out an offer to purchase the property. Once the offer is accepted by the seller, a contract is done up with the intent to buy, with a deadline to close. The person then markets and assigns the contract to another home buyer or investor. Once this is done, the wholesaler makes a profit, which is the difference between the contracted price with the seller and the amount paid by the new buyer—typically, $3,000 to $10,000 per home.

*The real estate wholesaling strategy is for example purposes only. Contact a real estate lawyer in your region to make sure there are no regional laws preventing such a strategy. When setting up a "conditional offer of sale contract" be sure to have it reviewed by a real estate professional prior to signing.

I get a few people who are stunned by this type of business and ask if it's even legal. It truly depends on the area, but the rule of thumb is if it's not specifically written that an "assignment cannot be made" in the agreement, then it can be done. The most important thing to remember with wholesaling is that if you're the wholesaler and can't find a new buyer, make sure to have enough exit clauses available in the agreement to be able to back out if you don't want or can't afford the property.

The last 2 ways to use real estate for investing is by renting or leasing a property. Some may complain that they don't want to deal with tenants, and I completely understand that. The best solution: hire a property management company! The goal is to invest without headaches and no work. Again, let professionals do what professionals do.

The goal with an income property is to gain rental income from rooms or units that will cover *all* the cost of the property, with built-in profit. Take note that I said ALL costs. That was my first mistake when I bought my first property; the rental income wasn't covering all costs, which made the property a liability (unless you foresee a massive increase in value in the near future).

It's best to make sure the income covers the expenses plus at least 5% for a maintenance buffer. Stuff wears and breaks, and being a landlord means it'll have to be replaced someday.

The benefits to renting out a property can be huge. Take my current home. I have restructured my mortgage to have the payments lowered to $1,600 per month. There's a two-bedroom finished apartment in my basement that I don't use. I rent this area out for $1,100 per month and have a side income investment that generates $300 per month in investment income. All in all, I only pay out of pocket $200 monthly for the mortgage, and $400 for utilities, insurance, and tax expenses.

Now, the other benefit is that since the tenants are paying the mortgage, I don't care about refinancing the home. Every year or two, I tap into any extra equity and principal repayment that's happened tax free. With these funds, I can then put into other higher gain investments.

As I mentioned earlier, not all debt is bad, and if the income you are receiving is covering the mortgage, what do you care about the interest rate? Borrow from the bank at 3%, and invest in a tax deferred account at 9%, so your overall gain is 6%, with little or no work from you.

Another type of income that you may take advantage of is income or gains received from property rights to films, television, music, books, and social media platforms. Unfortunately, due to time and space in this book, I will not be able to get into the specifics of each item; however, I wanted to bring them up as potential opportunities many rarely think of.

Firstly, the ownership rights of film, television, music, and literary works will typically come with some sort of residual pay on physical, digital, and now online streaming services sold around the world. This type of deal will happen if you are one of the primary creative elements, such as an actor, singer, director, writer, or producer on the project. Of course, the percentage of income will be on a product to product basis but is usually worked out in the initial contract, and always tied to sales.

Some might think you need to work on or have created the property to receive such a deal, but this is not always the case. Depending on the location in which the project is produced, and the agreement in the contract, the rights to properties like these can be bought and sold to different parties and can also be willed through an estate for a set length of time. In general, literary works published after 1977 will usually fall into the public domain 70 years after the death of the author.

Interesting fact: Dr Seuss passed away in 1991 and was rated #8 on Forbes' top dead celebrity list. His estate still earns a cool 16 million a year for selling children's books. Michael Jackson topped the list in 2017, at 75 million for his estate; he passed in 2009.

Now, probably the newest kid on the MSI list is social media. This is something that has come up in the last few years but has got traction thanks to the likes of Google and YouTube.

Pretty much anyone with a camera or even a smartphone can now create short videos, upload them online, and generate a decent amount of income from the number of subscribers and views a video gets. What started as a hobby for some can now be turned into a full-blown business.

The top income earners on YouTube are also not your average millionaires—far from it. Number 1 in 2018 was a 7-year-old boy named Ryan who reviews toys. He made a cozy $22 million under the channel name, Ryan's Toys Review.

Last year, it was reported he made $11 million from his channel, coming in at number 8 on Forbes' 2017 list, but the toy critic is moving on up. His YouTube channel attracts a large following from parents and children who watch Ryan test out new toys and share his thoughts.

Ryan, whose last name has currently not been made public, first started reviewing toys in 2015 when he was only **4 years old.** He was inspired by watching other kids and programs on YouTube and just wanted to join the fun. His most-watched video as of this writing features large Easter eggs and a bouncy house, which has amassed over 1.6 billion views. His channel has over 25 billion views in total and 17 million people who have subscribed. It is also reported the boy also now has his own line of collectibles selling at Walmart.

So, no matter how insignificant you think your idea might be, take heed that with some persistence and a little resourcefulness, it can be turned into a multimillion-dollar revenue stream.

The last stream of income that I will be bringing up is the owning of an automated business venture. This includes businesses such as ATMs, network marketing organizations, and small to large business ownership. Take note that I used the word, *automated*. The idea of buying or investing in a business is so that you can free up time and not purchase a job. This is something that a lot of people mess up on.

I used to be in the franchise business, working for the corporate overhead, and am also currently tied with a network marketing organization. I spoke to franchisee after franchisee who were under the impression that the businesses they invested in were to generate passive income, only to realize the profit margins were too small, and they ended up having to work at the business full time or more.

Don't get me wrong; if you enjoy and love working in whatever field you're investing in, then by all means go for it. I find it very hard to believe that someone enjoys slaving in a fast food kitchen for odd hours of the day, over and over when short staffed. My firm belief is that life is too short. Do what you really love. If you don't love it, then don't do it; pay someone else to do what they love.

If you do intend to invest in a multiple level network company, or a small or large business such as a franchise, make sure you're familiar with the services being offered and that the systems are in place to make the structure and training automatic. Understanding the costs and expenses that go along with the business to determine your profit margins and long-term potential prior to investing are also an important aspect. If you can't figure it out or fully understand it yourself, speak with multiple people in the industry to get a background view, and always get the advice from a lawyer and an accountant from a legal and financial standpoint.

The rule of thumb is that the annual take home revenue should be enough to cover the expense of management to run the business, with enough left over to give yourself a decent living once things are up and running.

I once knew a man who owned a 7/11 convenience store. He stated he initially thought the store was a good investment as it had steady income, but that he was always tired as he had to constantly open and close the store himself. He had been doing this for the last 10 years and barely had anytime to spend with his wife and kids. I asked him why he didn't hire a manager to run the store for him. He responded that the income wasn't good enough, and if he spent any money on additional staff, he would be underwater. I told him he purchased a job then.

Initially, he didn't like this idea, but then I broke it down for him. He was taking home roughly $50,000 annually after taxes. If you calculate the time spent in his store—from 7am till 11pm, Monday through Saturday (Sunday was his only day off), 16-hour days, 6 days a week—this equals 96 hours. Now, if you take his annual take home and divide by 52 weeks in the year, you get $961.53 per week. If you divide that amount by the 96 hours he put in, it equals only $10.02 cents per hour after tax. That puts it far below the current minimum wage of $14.00 in Ontario, Canada, with the current income tax deductions averaging roughly $10.92. That is why trading time for income is never a good bet. There's only so much time you can put into a day.

Now, I'm not saying 7/11 is not a good investment as at the time I didn't investigate the specifics of the deal. What I am saying is that if you're going to invest to buy a business, check and double check that the business is profitable enough to incur management costs. You hire the managers to run the business, and you look for ways to make more money with your money. This is the goal of the truly wealthy.

Sir Richard Branson's Virgin group owns a total of 400 different companies! It would be literally impossible to personally manage and run that many different people. You would go insane in a day. How do you think he does it? His philosophy, after reading his autobiography and doing some studying on him, is that he hires and surrounds himself with people who care and share his vision. Keep that in mind and see how you can grow.

With all these ideas for MSIs, keep in mind that all the above are simplistic examples. If you want to be successful, be as knowledgeable about a topic as you can. There are plenty of resources that can really expand your base knowledge about investing farther than I can in this book. Look around and find someone who has been successful in that field, and copy what they did till you get the same or similar results.

Exercise #7

Make a list of potential MSIs. Take a piece of paper or use the WINKs page. Write down at least 3 areas in which you can make passive $$$. Remember that these areas should not be J.O.B.'s, but only areas that would allow you to make additional money with little or no effort. Once you have the list, write 2 simple actions beside each one, which you can take towards making those a reality. The actions can be as simple as researching books on investing, or setting up a YouTube channel. Keep this list and review it monthly. Once an action has been completed, check it off. Write down another action in its place, and keep going to see where it takes you and how much you can grow!

Now, to find out how to protect all your assets from potential financial Armageddon, continue reading Chapter 8. This is where having proper shielding protection, when used properly, can be a powerful financial sword.

W.I.N.Ks

_____

_____

_____

_____

_____

_____

_____

_____

_____

_____

_____

_____

_____

_____

_____

Chapter 8
Insurance, So What?

"Do something today that your future self will thank you for."
— Sean Patrick Flanery

These days, we have all kinds of protection, don't we? We buy insurance to protect our car, our house, and even our smartphone, but when it comes to protecting one's life and family, it's generally not taken seriously. It's unfortunate these days that people are still very skeptical about insurance for themselves and their loved ones. As a result, most people don't have any life insurance, or not enough.

I know life insurance is not a fun topic to discuss, but it's something that must be brought up if you want to build long-term wealth and preserve that wealth for future generations.

The way I view financial stability is like the structure of a house. When building a strong, sturdy home, you always need a proper foundation at the base. Proper insurance is that foundation for your financial home. If a wind storm or flood comes along without a proper foundation, your home easily gets decimated, and it's almost impossible to rebuild. Having that foundation gives the stability and security that even if most of your home is destroyed, it's easier to rebuild because of it.

The common misconception is that life insurance insures your life. It really insures your family's ability to endure without being financially wiped out.

The problem stems, I believe, from the belief that most people have about death. Unless something happens to them around the concept of death, most people rarely consider that it could happen to them anytime soon. Everyone truly believes they will live a long, healthy life, so why would they need life insurance?

Another issue could probably be the bad presumptions people have in dealing with certain insurance companies and their payout histories.

Case in point is mortgage insurance. I have heard client after client speak of mortgage insurance as if it's life insurance, and get upset when something happens and the bank doesn't pay. They paid all this money for years, and when something bad happened, they didn't receive any benefit.

When a bank asks for that extra insurance premium of a few dollars a month added on to your mortgage in case something happens, it is just **credit protection**. Very few people realize that this insurance places the bank as the beneficiary of the insurance payout, not your family.

The other problem is that they do what is called underwriting at the time of claim. This means they accept everyone initially, regardless of health, age, or medical history, and give everyone the same rate. Now, when it comes time to make a claim, the insurance company has people called underwriters who research and make sure everything is up to their standards regarding a claim. They can literally find the smallest thing from your history to deny the claim.

When doing the math, getting a separate term policy would be far more beneficial and cheaper to protect an asset like your home, assuming you don't have any major health concerns.

Now, some people also just take it easy by signing up for their employer's insurance plan. You don't need to have any medical checkup, and you might even get it for free. The problem here is that you may not be adequately covered, and if your employment is ever terminated, or you're laid off, the coverage stops. You may also find it difficult to get individual coverage if you have medical issues or require more coverage.

Now, the question to ask is, are you insurable? Most life insurance requires a medical exam with blood tests, urine samples, and medical history before a policy can be issued. If you have a health concern, the company could deny your application or give you a *rated*, higher premium fee. Thus, in regard to getting your insurance, you should get it as young as possible. This way, you are less likely to run into health being an issue, and you may also qualify for lower premiums.

A high percentage of people in Canada and the United States are not even insurable, and don't even know it. With the rise of cancers, heart disease, strokes, and diabetes hitting almost epidemic levels, you need to be aware of your own health status and how it affects your insurability.

There are some policies that can be issued without a medical exam. These are called **guaranteed issue**; however, these policies come with higher premium rates and lower coverage.

Many people I speak with are still confused as to how insurance cost actually works. Buying insurance is no different than any other thing you buy day to day. For example, a ticket to the movie theatre, as of this writing, costs roughly $12, and a dozen eggs costs roughly $2, so insurance is charged based on COI (cost of insurance) units for every $1,000 of coverage. Those units can vary in price depending on multiple factors, such as age, gender, and current and past medical history, and this cost will only increase with age—similar to the way auto insurance companies rate their customers based on driving history.

Now, some believe only the bread winners or families need insurance, but single individuals and stay-at-home parents also require protection. Think about all the jobs a stay-a-home parent is required to do: cooking, cleaning, accounting, looking after the kids, and driving, among many other daily tasks. Without the stay-at-home parent, it can sometimes cost just as much or more to replace them to keep the family going.

For the single individual, they might have different reasons to be insured, like the following:

- They want to take advantage of saving in a policy that has tax deferred growth with coverage at the same time.
- They may have debts that have a co-signer that they don't want to burden.
- They may want to start a family soon and take advantage of the lower cost.
- They may have loved ones like parents or siblings to care for.
- They may want to leave a legacy to a charity or cause they may truly believe in.

Whatever the reason, it's best to know your own insurance needs.

Business owners require different types of insurance, such as **key person insurance** and **overhead expense coverage,** which protects you, the owner, in the event of losing a key person such as a manager, or dealing with overhead costs should you have to deal with being disabled in the future.

The way financial consultants deal with insurance needs is by calculating the **DIME Method**. DIME stands for debt, income, mortgage, and education. It's an easy formula that is designed to cover your financial responsibilities.

Example of a hypothetical situation

Example of a hypothetical situation
Client

Debt	$25,000(Combined debts including credit cards and loans.)
Income	$480,000($4k/mo. Income replacement for 10 years.)
Mortgage	$250,000(Current mortgage balances.)
Education	$80.000(Assuming $20k/yr. for 4-years university for 1 child.)
TOTAL	**$835,000 Insurance Need**

With $835,000 of coverage, if this person passes away early, the surviving spouse will have enough funds to cover all the current debts, including their mortgage. Also, they will have enough income for the next 10 years, and to pay for their child's 4-year university education.

The thing to keep in mind is that this is their current insurance need, and obviously this would change over time, like their mortgage and debts being paid off. Therefore, it is recommended every year or 2 to re-evaluate your insurance needs to make sure you are properly covered.

Other potential insurance needs should also be taken into consideration, such as final expenses like funeral costs, estate taxes, and leaving a legacy. These items will be discussed in a following chapter.

The question some people ask is, "Which is better for me, term or permanent insurance?" That depends; what are you protecting? You should first get a clear understanding between the two types. Being general in nature, these concepts work equally well in the United States and Canada.

Term Insurance is what it implies. You are protected for a set time period, or *term*, of 1, 5, 10, 20, or even 30 years in length. At the end of the term, the coverage ceases, unless it is available to renew for another term, which will come with higher premiums or convert to a permanent insurance policy. Even a group employer insurance policy can be converted to an individual policy when leaving. Most often, this privilege typically ends 31 days after leaving the employer. The cost for term starts off cheaper when you are young but becomes drastically more expensive with age, as your risk of dying is higher the older you get.

The primary purpose is to have protection for a set period of time, such as to cover outstanding debts or take care of loved ones such as children. With that in mind, some people feel it's a good idea to have **decreasing term insurance**. Typically sold as mortgage insurance, the premium cost will not increase during the life of the mortgage. Since the mortgage goes down every year, the benefit paid out from the policy will decrease every year as well. Be sure to double check the cost of this. It's sometimes better to have a level term plan, as the benefit paid out will remain constant and not decrease during the term.

The primary downside and a common complaint to term insurance is that if nothing happens during the term, all the premiums paid are gone. This is were **Permanent Insurance** comes in. Often considered Term + cash, this is where you have the insurance policy for your entire life. Now, instead of just paying for the insurance part, a portion of the premium is set aside into a cash value, which you can access while you are living or increase the benefit.

There are two kinds of permanent insurance: **Whole Life (WL)** and **Universal Life (UL)**. Whole life is the oldest form of cash value insurance. You will pay higher premiums, which are fixed, but these policies will generally give a guaranteed rate of interest on the cash value.

Some insurance companies offer what is called participating plans. These WL plans allow the plan owners to become shareholders of the company and will pay dividends, but the dividends are not guaranteed.

A common objection people give when discussing WL plans is, "Why not buy term and invest the rest?" The idea theorizes if I pay $2,000 per year for a Whole life policy, why not just buy a Term plan for $400 a year, and the other $1,600 put into another investment (like a mutual fund) to get a better rate of return. There are some believers in this theory. Some even convert their plans from WL to Term.

For this scenario to work, you need to A) have the proper discipline to invest the difference consistently. If not, you might just end up buying a Term plan and spending the rest, and B) you must know where to invest and be willing to accept what the market gives you. Other investments could give you a better rate of return but could also have the chance of wiping out your entire nest egg.

Universal Life (UL) is the next option that has come up to give consumers more flexibility. Like Whole Life plans, UL plans are intended to give coverage for your entire life and accumulate a cash value. The primary differences are that you have a variety of investment options for the cash value, which could potentially give higher returns, and there is more flexibility in the premium payments. There are even options in the United States to have your plan indexed, and track the return of a specific index, like the S&P 500. When the plan is being set up, the plan provider will outline the minimum and maximum premiums you could pay into the plan.

The big benefit is that UL policies can be a useful tool for implementing some tax and/or estate strategies. These will vary based on area and time, so always make sure to discuss such strategies with your financial planner and/or tax accountant.

Segregated Funds (or individual variable insurance contracts) are another option to Canadians. They combine investments, such as mutual funds, with a life insurance contract to offer various guarantees. The type of guarantee will promise that you will receive a minimum portion of your initial investment or market value (whichever is higher) after a set period of 10-15 years or death. 10-year terms typically come with a 75% principle guarantee, whereas the death benefit is usually 100%. This means if your funds have an abysmal return and drop 80%, and if you wait out the term, you're guaranteed to get at least 75% of your initial investment back. At any time, the term can also be reset to take advantage of any growth in the market, so if the value goes up, you can lock in the growth and set it aside for another 10 years. Segregated funds may also provide protection from creditors and avoid estate taxes upon death.

As for additional customization, there are also various add-ons to policies, called ***Riders.*** These are generally cheaper to add to an existing policy than to have as an individual plan. Some types of available riders are accidental death and dismemberment, disability, critical illness, and return of premiums, to name a few.

So, what to choose? Term, WL, UL, or Seg Fund? All have pros and cons, but it all breaks down to your needs and goals for your financial future. At the end of the day, there's no free lunch when it comes to insurance. You'll have to pay for it. Determine what you want to gain and what you want to avoid, and work backwards to figure out what's going to get you there.

Just remember, it's always best to review any product with your insurance agent to help navigate all the features and options.

Now, under the current rules laid out by the Internal Revenue Service (IRS), and the Canada Revenue Agency (CRA), insurance policies receive many tax advantages. This is the best kept secret of the wealthy. Remember, I mentioned earlier one of the keys to building wealth is to be as tax efficient as possible. Any investment vehicle that gives tax advantages is to be cherished.

First off, any death benefit received from an insurance policy is tax-free for the beneficiaries, and this also includes the cash value built up inside the policy.

Next, all additional earnings and growth inside the policy get tax deferred growth. This means, if you have a WL or UL policy, any extra interest, growth, or dividends earned are not taxed until either you decide to cancel the policy (called a surrender), the policy has lapsed for missed payments, or when excessive distributions occur.

Finally, you can take advantage of tax-free withdrawals or loans. Withdrawals can made from the cash value up to the adjusted cost base without being taxed. This is the amount of money that was personally paid into the policy for premiums using your after-tax dollars.

Besides withdrawals, tax-free policy loans can be made above your cost basis to give you greater access to funds. When you take a loan from the insurance company or another lender, they will take the amount from your cash value and put it in a separate account. The lender is then entitled to get paid back the amount of the loan, and uses the death benefit as collateral should you not pay it back. Keep in mind, these loans charge interest, so you need to consider if that works into your financial strategy.

For the IRS, as long as you stay within their guidelines, loans and withdrawals can be taken without any tax liability.

For Canadians, the CRA allows favorable tax treatment for insurance policies. Every scenario is different, so be sure to consult a tax professional and insurance agent when dealing with your specific policy.

So, the final question about life insurance is, "At what age is the best to get it?" My honest answer: YESTERDAY!! You can really benefit from insurance at any age for different reasons.

Even children as young as 30 days old can have a policy set up. Obviously, the child doesn't require a large death benefit, as their responsibilities are very low, and they probably don't have any bills or debt yet; so, a new way of thinking is that a WH or UL policy is a great way to start an early savings plan for your child, and it is inexpensive. Remember, the younger they are, the cheaper it is, and the plans come with some great tax perks as well.

Most WH policies have the option to pay the plan down early, and can even be funded within 20 years or less. So, effectively, you can have a WH policy fully funded by the time the child goes to college or university. The tax-free loans or withdrawals from the built-up cash value is super effective for using on anything from paying for secondary education, buying a car, or even a down payment on a house. The options and strategies are almost endless.

Just remember, no matter what route you go, insurance is an integral part of any good financial plan, and when used properly, can be a sharp sword in your financial arsenal.

Exercise #8

Do the DIME method on yourself and your family to determine your insurance needs. Are you properly covered? If not, set up an appointment with an insurance broker to get a free insurance assessment. I always advise speaking with brokers as opposed to an individual insurance company, as brokers will have wider access to various providers, which will save you time shopping around. Some questions to ask the broker are how long they've been in business, how many providers they deal with, and how they are compensated. Make sure all the pros and cons are clearly laid out for any product shown. Don't always base a product on price alone, as sometimes different providers will have different perks that may benefit your situation more. Make sure you're comparing apples to apples.

So, to see how to take care of your loved ones once you're gone, and leave a great lasting legacy, continue reading on to Act 3.

W.I.N.Ks

Act 3

You've Changed, Now What???

Chapter 9
It All Comes to an End

"If today were the last day of my life, would I want to do what I'm doing? When the answer has been "NO" too many days in a row, I know something needs to change."
– Steve Jobs

Congratulations! You have made it to the final act. If you've managed to complete all the exercises throughout this book, you're well on your way to upgrading your financial destiny.

Now, there is one last piece of the financial puzzle that needs to be told. How can you preserve your wealth and leave a lasting legacy after you've passed on? I know it's not the most fun or entertaining topic, but it is an important one as no one truly knows when they will pass on.

It's an unfortunate fact that in Canada and the United States we pay some of the highest tax rates in the world. This is what gives us a higher quality of life, but when you think about it: you eat, you pay taxes; you buy stuff, you pay taxes; you work, you pay more taxes! The list is endless. Another event in your life, which most people don't consider, is that even when you die, you pay taxes! That's right; there's this little thing called estate taxes, and if you're not prepared, the government can walk away with **up to almost 50%** of your final assets, and good luck trying to argue and fight it, as you'll be six feet under.

Now, I know most people might come up with the initial excuse of, "Well, Ryan, I'm dead; what do I care if I pay more in taxes after I'm gone?" Well, you should care. This is your hard-earned money that could be better used towards helping your relatives in a tough time, or even a good cause that you'd like to support.

Just take the late, great singer, Prince, for example. He passed away in 2016, without an estate plan or a Will prepared, with an estimated estate valued at over 200 million dollars. Just two years later, as of this writing, his heirs have not yet received a single penny from his estate.

Don't get me wrong; people have been getting paid—just not the ones you'd think. So far, only the executor, lawyers, accountants, and advisors have been paid anything, and it adds up to a sum of close to 10 million dollars thus far for fees and expenses. When it's all said and done (which could take several more years), the IRS and the state of Minnesota could be getting a nice estate payday of close to 100 million dollars! This could have easily been avoided with a Will.

To top it off, you might not be aware that if you happen to pass away without a Will, you'll have died **intestate,** and your estate will move into the position of **probate**. The definition of probate is "the judicial process by which a decedent's estate is valued, beneficiaries are determined, an executor in charge of estate distribution is declared, and the estate is legally transferred to the determined beneficiaries."

So, in simple terms, the courts and the government have the underlying task of determining all final decisions of your financial assets and property, and this includes your children. Let me say that again. The government will decide and make the final decision on who raises your children should you pass away with dependants who can't yet support themselves. This process is generally very lengthy and can take several years to finalize.

The first misconception is that if you pass away without a Will, your spouse will assume and take control of everything. This, unfortunately, is not the case. Firstly, the estate will go through the probate process and taxes are paid.

Next, any creditors that still might be owing are paid off. The probate process has the downside of being also open to public view. This means that anyone has knowledge to the funds that are remaining in your estate. This is where scam and con artists make their move to either a fraudulent creditor claim or waiting for a window where you're alone and vulnerable. Either one can cause extreme difficulties during an already overly difficult time.

Once all that has been cleared, all remaining funds are distributed by how the courts deem fit, and the estate is closed.

As for property, it depends on the state or province, but generally, if the marital property was setup as *joint ownership*, the surviving spouse takes full ownership; however, if the property was setup as *tenancy in common*, someone else could receive that portion of the home, which could be a nightmare to deal with.

So, how do you create a Will? The process is easier than you think. There are numerous free Will templates that can be downloaded off the internet that can get you started at creating a basic Will. Go to **www.moneymagnetpath.com** and download one from the free bonus section.

The main items to think about when creating a basic Will are:

A) The Executor: this person will be responsible for arranging the funeral, securing and appraising all assets, paying off all debts and taxes, and finally, contacting and distributing all remaining funds to heirs.

B) Heirs of your financial assets: who will get what after you die.

C) Guardian of any children or dependants: who will take care of them until they are of legal age.

An important note: whoever you choose should be aware and agree to the guardianship. Some people may be too concerned with their own lives to be guardians of your children. If they decide not to become guardians, your children would be given to the local municipality, and their fate decided by the courts. The most obvious choice would be your spouse, but to really be prepared, you should have 2 or 3 backups for the worst-case scenario of you and your spouse both dying in an accident, like a car crash.

Now, if people you know are hesitant to be potential guardians of your children should the worst happen, you can always ease their mind a bit that you have insurance coverage to cover the children until they reach 18 years old. This will alleviate one of their stresses, as they're usually either taken aback by the mental or financial responsibility of it all.

D) Assess and divide your property: make sure any items you own, such as paintings, electronics, jewelry, and even real estate, are accounted for, and who it goes to is clearly defined.

E) Sign the Will, and be sure to clearly date and sign with at least 2 competent witnesses. The purpose of the witness is to confirm that it was you who signed the Will. To be valid, the witnesses should be at least 18 years old and not be a beneficiary on the Will.

Now, contrary to the idea, you do not have to have your Will notarized. A lawyer does not have to write your Will, and most people do not need a lawyer's help to make a basic Will, one that leaves a home, investments, and personal items to your loved ones, and, if you have young children, that names a guardian to take care of them.

The only time a lawyer may be required is if you have extensive complicated assets such as businesses and/or multiple real estate properties.

Once this is done, you should store your Will in a safety deposit box. Because the executor will need the original Will to handle your affairs efficiently, a Will should be stored in a safe and accessible place, and the executor should know exactly where it is kept and how to get it.

So, what happens if you get into a situation where you're not dead but incapacitated and unable to give commands for how you'd like to be treated? In comes the **Living Will**, a written statement detailing your desires regarding your medical treatment in situations where you are no longer able to express informed consent. This could be in situations such as a coma or brain damage.

A sad story that hit the news recently was of a family who was fighting the courts in Ontario, Canada to keep their 27-year-old daughter on life support. After the woman survived a drug overdose, she went into a coma, and doctors claimed the brain damage was too extensive to ever heal. After a year of being on life support, a judge finally ruled that she was to be taken off life support, as multiple doctors claimed she would never recover. Due to the fact there was no Living Will in place, the family had no choice in the matter.

Lastly, there's the final basic issue of handling or closing any of your accounts should you pass away or become incapacitated and unable to give commands. This can be exceptionally difficult with the absence of a **Power of Attorney**. Such things as a cell phone bill, a hydro bill, mortgage, and even bank accounts cannot be controlled or closed unless the account was set up as joint. This means the surviving spouse would have to wait until the court passes it through probate, and they get approval to be able to take control of certain utilities or bills.

The process to setting up a Living Will and a Power of Attorney vary depending on your state or province, so you should double check local requirements. A Living Will does not require a lawyer and is like a Will; however, a Power of Attorney does need to be notarized, and some areas require the document to be on file in the local land records office.

As you age, and as your financial situation changes over the years, it's important to make sure your documents are kept up to date.

The last thing you want is to go through an ugly divorce and forget to update your Will, only to have your ex-spouse claim your estate when you die, when all you wanted was for everything to go to your current spouse. It can be an uncomfortable but avoidable situation.

Beneficiaries are also something that must be monitored and updated on insurance policies and accounts regularly. Ideally, you should also have 2 or more contingent beneficiaries in place just in case one should pre-decease you.

Now, you might ask about underage or uncapable beneficiaries, like children. When making your final arrangements with your planner, you should really consider the competency of all your beneficiaries. Ideally, for these situations, arranging to have a **Trust** set up is the most convenient method. This is were a trustee is appointed to manage that trust until a determined age, such as 25 or longer. Various assets can be put into trusts, including real estate, stocks, and bonds. There are various types of trusts available, depending on your needs, such as a living trust, testamentary trust, revocable trust, irrevocable trust, and funded or unfunded. When you have more assets and are looking for the safest, most tax efficient ways to preserve your wealth, trusts are an excellent option.

The benefits to trusts are that you can determine how the funds will be issued in advance. You can have monthly payments made up until a desired age and then have the funds fully issued, or just have the payment postponed until a set date.

For beneficiaries who are not underage and fully competent, but perhaps someone who is just not responsible with their money or parent you may need to care for, another option would be to set up an investment called an **Annuity**. An annuity is a contract where payments or a lump sum is given directly to an insurance company. In exchange, payments are made back to the annuitant for a set number of years or for life, with a guaranteed rate of interest. This is useful when someone like a spouse requires monthly income to cover their expenses but has a tough time handling their finances.

Other than that, just doing a quick checkup every year or two on these items should suffice to keep things in order.

Now, with all this hard work and effort to make and create wealth, you might think, "What's it all for?" Well, to start, you making wealth does not help me much. It helps you for a finite amount of time as you can only spend and enjoy so much while you're in this world. What it really does is gives you a vessel to creating lasting generational wealth for you to leave behind a legacy.

A legacy is something that you can leave behind for future generations to continue building onto the wealth you've created, and it doesn't always have to be money. Just educating your children and teaching them the laws of finance is also an important part.

One of the most important keys to improving any skill is the ability to teach that skill to others. Not only are you strengthening these concepts in your own mind, but you are also helping to develop the minds of others, especially your children.

Some of the worst stories that can be heard are of children born wealthy who had it all and either blew or lost all their parents' inheritance. This is something that could have easily been avoided had those parents taken the time to educate and instill proper values in them.

Another great way to leave a legacy of value is by leaving a part of your estate to a charity or a cause you truly believe in. This has a great two-tier effect of not only helping those in need, but it can reduce, and in some situations, eliminate, the estate tax liability upon death.

If you leave something to charity in your Will to a set limit, then it won't count towards the total taxable value of your estate. This is called leaving a **Charitable Legacy**.

This is a way to be remembered not only by your loved ones but by the people you helped. Just imagine your tombstone and the sentence under your name. What does it say to describe you and your life? Is it something good, like, "Here lies *so and so*, a brave warm-hearted individual who lived and died to help others," or does it say something not so nice, like, "Here lies *so and so*; he lived and had a lot of money." Either way, the choice is up to you how that sentence will eventually be written.

When making your final preparations, always speak with an estate planner. This way you can find out the most tax efficient and easiest way to truly leave the legacy you want.

So, when is the best time to prepare for your end? To be honest, YESTERDAY! Especially if you have children who rely on you. Even if you don't have that much in the way of assets, you should always have something in writing just in case your end should come.

Nobody knows when their number is up. Nobody wants to think about it, but everyone will have to go through it at some point. At least if you're prepared and have all your affairs in order, it'll be one less stress for you, and one less giant stress for your loved ones.

To recap, the 4 primary reasons you need a Will are:

1. Having a Will makes it much easier for your family or friends to sort everything out when you pass on.

2. If you don't write a Will, everything you own will be shared out in a standard way defined by the law, which isn't always the way you might want.

3. A Will can help reduce the amount of tax that might be payable on the value of the property and money you leave behind, or if you want to leave something to people outside your immediate family.

4. Writing a Will is important if you have children or other family members who depend on you for guardianship; not having a Will means the government decides who will take care of them.

With all this knowledge, take heed that you'll have taken a massive step in securing your wealth, and trust that your legacy will live on in many generations to come.

Exercise #9

Draft a Will, Living Will, and a Power of Attorney for yourself and your spouse. Go to **www.moneymagnetpath.com** and download a free, basic Will template to get started. After you and your spouse have written your Wills, contact an estate planner in your area to arrange getting a Living Will and a Power of Attorney completed under local requirements. Once these are completed, keep them somewhere safe, such as a safety deposit box.

Now, to find out how to take your finances by the metaphorical balls, continue reading Chapter 10: Who Needs a Coach? Here, I explain the benefits of getting advice from professionals, and what to look for in one.

W.I.N.Ks

Chapter 10
Who Needs a Coach?

"To understand a man, you must first walk a mile in his moccasins."
– North American Indian Proverb

To be great with your finances, you need a coach to help you along the way. Like being physically fit, your chances of success skyrocket when someone is there to guide and support you.

I once heard an interesting story. There was a large auto manufacturing plant in a small American town. This plant had some of the best and newest machinery to produce some of the latest cars. It also happened to be the largest employer in the town, as it employed thousands of workers who worked around the clock on multiple shifts. This plant was so good that it consistently held the top position in the company as being the most efficient, as everyone knew their job and did it well.

One day, out of nowhere, the machines and the assembly lines suddenly stopped working. Everyone was shocked, and they froze, as this had never happened before. The management and service team looked and looked but could not find anything that would cause the lines to stop running.

Of course, the main plant manager was getting extremely frustrated because, with all the labor and expenses, this setback was easily costing the plant hundreds of dollars every second the lines were down.

After an hour of inspecting and being unable to find the problem, the plant manager relented and called a local mechanic to come take a look.

The mechanic quickly arrived and walked up to one of the larger electrical panels. He opened it, only to see a bee's nest of wires, plugs, and screws. The mechanic quickly looked over the panel, took out a wrench, placed the wrench on a single screw, and turned the screw half a turn. Suddenly, like magic, the plant lit up, and all the machines started running again!

Ecstatic, the plant manager thanked the mechanic and asked him for the bill, and said he would pay him right away. The mechanic said, "Okay," looked around, and grabbed a piece of paper off the closest table. He wrote something on the paper and handed it back to the manager.

The manager looked up in shock and said, "ARE YOU SERIOUS? A THOUSAND DOLLARS! This is outrageous. You were here for less than 10 minutes, and you only turned one screw. I need an itemized list of what's being charged."

The mechanic said, "Okay," took back the paper, wrote a few more things on it, and handed it back to the manager.

The plant manager looked at the paper, nodded his head, pulled out a check book immediately, and wrote the mechanic a check for the amount.

After the mechanic left, a mid-level manager went up the plant manager and asked him, "What did the mechanic write?" The plant manager gave him the paper. He looked down, and it read:

Services to be Rendered
$1.00 – Turning screw
$999.00 – Knowing which screw to turn
Total: $1,000.00

It's a story I've heard from many different people, but one that really drives the point down about paying for proper knowledge.

After studying so many successful individuals in different fields, over the last decade, I have discovered a common trait among them. Every single one of them had a mentor and coaches, and all them got advice from people who were more knowledgeable and more experienced about a specific topic than they were.

This has led me to believe if you want to be great at something, find someone who's good at it and learn how they did it.

Some might wonder what the difference between coaching and mentoring is, and it really boils down to the relationship.

Coaching is something that occurs in the short term and is field specific, like a basketball coach. Mentoring is usually long term, going on for several years, and gets into deeper aspects of growth and development. Thus, someone typically will build a stronger relationship with their mentor.

A large percentage of people, business owners, and entrepreneurs don't get mentors or coaches. The idea behind this is because they feel it's a sign of weakness or a waste of resources, but this is a big misconception. People with mentors and coaches show they are willing to learn, are open to different perspectives, and are adaptable to change. This tip alone can literally save you years of stress and aggravation, much like the factory not knowing what little screw to turn. You'd figure, since star athletes always have a super coach behind them, why not you?

Even the entrepreneur legend, Sir Richard Branson, who now owns over 400 companies, credits his success to one of his early mentors. Branson asked British airline entrepreneur, Sir Freddie Laker, for direction during his struggle to get Virgin Atlantic Airlines flying.

Branson wrote in the British newspaper, *The Sun*: "*It's always good to have a helping hand at the start. I wouldn't have got anywhere in the airline industry without the mentorship of Sir Freddie Laker.*"

Unfortunately, not all coaches are created equal, and there are a few proven ways to help you seek out a coach that will get you the results you want and deserve.

First off, check their credentials and credibility. What's their professional designation? Degrees, diplomas, or any government licences? Find out their education or what training they did. Also, are they with any professional affiliations, such as organizations they might currently belong to?

Next, you need to determine their level of expertise. How long have they been in the field, and is this length of experience adequate for your needs? What area do they specialize in? Most coaches, even in the personal finance space, will specialize in a specific area, such as small business owners.

Is contacting any of their past clients possible? References are best verified and checked. Be ready with questions, as this will give you a good birds-eye view on how the coach works and deals with clients.

If possible, try and get a sample session from the coach. Most will offer a first meeting for free, and this gives you an opportunity to give the coach a test run.

On your first meeting, the things to take note of are A) Did you feel comfortable with the coach, and did the session meet your needs? B) Were you the focus, or did the coach spend too much time on themselves? C) Did you go to the session with a topic, and was it met during the meeting?

Now, there could be a chance that getting a coach or mentor isn't in the cards for you right now. Don't fret, as you can still be mentored. There are many books on successful people and how they became successful.

This was how I started my educational journey. Reading books on people like Arnold Schwarzenegger, Steve Jobs, Oprah, and Sir Richard Branson really opens your eyes and will give you a different outlook on how to accomplish goals in your life, especially when it comes to money.

The side bonus of reading about these highly successful individuals is that not only do you learn from them, you will also be super inspired by the ups and downs they went through, only to realize they are normal people just like you and me. This gives you the best thing of all: Belief.

Business titans, sports stars, and even famous actors leverage the knowledge, expertise, and unique skills of professional coaches. A coach is your sounding board, your confidant, and your safe place to expand and explore. They're there to challenge you and see you in ways perhaps you take for granted or cannot see yourself yet. They're working with you to meet your goals, holding you accountable, and supporting you when you fall. They're also your champion and cheerleader, standing beside you, celebrating you and your wins. Coaches can be your secret silent partner, tucked away in your back pocket.

The important thing to remember about having a mentor or coach is to listen clearly and do EVERYTHING they say, and I mean everything! Even if it doesn't make sense at first.

A lot of people I've worked with over the years, who've tried coaches, fall into 1 of 3 categories. The first category hears what the coach says, and they say, "Okay, that sounds great," and then never take any action beyond that. Surprise, surprise, they get lousy results. All that comes from them is excuses as to why they couldn't accomplish what they wanted.

Next, there are the ones who hear their coach and verbally say, "Okay, fine," but internally, in their head, they say to themselves, "This won't work; this guy doesn't know what he's talking about; I'm going to do my own thing." After which, again, they get bad results. This time around, they do the blame game on the coach's training, followed by aggression that the coach gave bad advice, and they completely avoid taking any responsibility—even though they didn't follow through with anything that was instructed, or attempted it haphazardly.

The third and final person is one who takes full responsibility and initiative to learn and practise everything they can. This person realizes the coach has some knowledge to give, and they take everything as gospel.

This is how I was when I first got into door-to-door sales. At the time, I was a young guy and didn't know anything about sales or proper communication. What I did know is that I was a good learner and could hold up a conversation. So, when I witnessed my sales trainer make more money in one day than I was making in an entire month, I was hooked.

I picked his brain for every little detail, to the point I'm sure it annoyed him. Doing this had the effect that within a few months I was competing with him for sales and running for competitive bonuses.

This is where things really started to kick in for me. I quickly realized I could only gain so much info from this individual salesman, and I wanted more. Soon after, I walked in to the office of the VP of sales and asked him straight up who the top 3 salespeople were in the company. He, of course, told me, and for the following few weeks, I shadowed and hounded all 3 of them for every detail of how they did their craft.

I copied everything—how they did their pitch, how they spoke, how they handled their team, and even how they dressed. To me, if they were doing it and getting better results, then it should, in theory, give me similar results.

The effects of my efforts paid off. Within 2 years, I worked my way up to being one of the top most consistent sales reps. I won multiple company bonuses, and I eventually got promoted to an office manager before the company sold.

The experience and education I received from that position outdid any postsecondary education for life skills. Everything I learned was transferrable and aided me in every business venture after that.

What I truly believe about mentors and coaches is that they have experience. They went through the trial and errors for years, sometimes decades, before figuring it out. If you can take that same knowledge and learning curve, and condense it into a few days or weeks, you can completely change your life, faster and easier than you ever would trying it yourself. You can truly become the best version of yourself!

Now, being that you're now on the path to financial independence, it's safe to say you've probably started recording your path in the form of a financial statement or budget. If you haven't, you need to start. As I mentioned earlier, energy flows where the focus goes, so if you focus on your own financial statement, and record your progress, improvements will come.

It may take a few weeks or months to start seeing any results, but that's the way things are with a new skill. Take exercise or working out for example. Would you go to the gym only 3 times and get annoyed you didn't have a six-pack yet? Heck no, you'd realize it takes consistent action and discipline to get the results you wanted.

Journaling helps you with that. All successful people write down what they want, when they want it, and how they're doing on the journey.

I personally write down ideas and thoughts daily about my goals and vision. This helps me stay focused and keeps me on track.

Unfortunately, 95% of the population can't even take the time to write a goal, let alone track its progress. Then you wonder why only 2% of people are financially wealthy.

Once you start writing your goals and journaling about your progress, you'll start to notice patterns in your actions and results. Maybe certain tasks might account for a larger amount of your results. This is expected.

A little interesting concept I learned early in my sales career was **Pareto's Principle,** or the 80/20 rule. This law states that roughly 80% of effects comes from 20% of the causes, and this law has been found to translate into almost every aspect of life.

Named after the famed economist, Vilfred Pareto, it was originally used in Italy, and it was discovered that 20% of the population owned 80% of the land. From there, this law was applied and used for countless surveys, and was found to have connections to many more aspects, including finance.

Take the world GDP (gross domestic product) for example, in 1989: the richest 20% owned 82.7% of the world's wealth. For companies, it has been found 80% of sales comes from 20% of the clients. Even at social gatherings, surveys find 20% of guests will eat roughly 80% of the food.

So, how does this relate to you? With journaling, you will start to notice where your results come from. At that point, you want to cut out or reduce the other 80% of your actions. This in turn will increase your overall results.

For investing, you may find that 20% of your investments are generating close to 80% of your total returns. If that's the case, then focus more on the top 20, and reduce the other 80 to increase to have a better (ROI) return on investment.

Maybe you also find that you're spending only 20% of your career time on actual career building. That's a sign you need to evaluate what you're doing during your time that's not productive, and reduce or eliminate it. Regularly cutting out or reducing minimal tasks, such as email, Facebook, or coffee breaks, can have an almost magical difference on your daily production.

I applied this to my own life, and the results were astonishing. I even noticed I wore 20% of my wardrobe 80% of the time. This caused me to clean out my closet and donate almost half my clothes. It didn't help much financially, but my closet sure is clean and organized now!

Exercise #10

Find a mentor or pick someone successful to emulate. There are tons of options, but make sure the person is a true success in their field. If the person is an ultra success, like Sir Richard Branson, and harder to meet, try and find books that they wrote or are about them, such as autobiographies. This will give you an in-depth look at how they think. Most successful people are happy to share their knowledge, and it shouldn't be hard to gain a meeting with someone in your chosen field.

There are also quite a few coaches out there online that charge for their knowledge. I personally endorse paying for knowledge. One of my mentors I subscribe to is **Raymond Aaron's Monthly Mentor program**. He's a *New York Times* bestselling author and international public speaker, and he has worked wonders for me. If you can gain info for free, and use it, that's great, but typically, a person will cherish the knowledge they gain more if they must put something out for it.

Now, to find out how to take full control of the most important aspect to building true wealth— your mental state—continue reading Chapter 11. Here, I explain how our mental states can hinder or benefit us, and what you can do to take control.

W.I.N.Ks

_____

_____

_____

_____

_____

_____

_____

_____

_____

_____

_____

_____

_____

_____

_____

_____

Chapter 11
Thermometer or Thermostat?

"It is in your moments of decision that your destiny is shaped"
— Tony Robbins

Now, as I'm writing this, it's the middle of winter in Ontario, Canada. For those that know and have been there, it gets cold, and there's a lot of snow. It's beautiful looking at it when you're inside and warm, but rather uncomfortable when you're out in it, unless you're prepared. As I look out my window at my beautiful backyard in the early morning, I'm reminded of a descriptive comparison about success. I initially heard it through the business entrepreneur, Ed Mylett, and it's whether you can act like a thermometer or a thermostat.

You're probably wondering what that means. Well, what does a thermometer do? It tells you what the temperature is, and nothing more. It reacts to its environment and reflects the results. That's how most people go through life. They react to whatever life gives them. If it gets cold in their life, like they lose their job, lose someone close to them, or an investment doesn't do well, they show it and get down. If their life happens to get warm and results get better, they're happy. They chalk it up to luck or good fortune. They believe life is happening to them, not for them.

On the flip side, what does a thermostat do? It's a regulator of the temperature. If you open the doors and windows in the middle of winter, and a breeze of ice-cold air enters the home, the internal temperature will drop. What happens next? The thermostat kicks in and works its butt off to bring the temperature back to 22 Celsius, or 72 Fahrenheit, whichever you use. The real trick is to start setting your internal temperature high, so even if you don't hit it, you'll be better off than most people around you.

What happens if your heating system gets slow or breaks down? Do you sit around, whine, and complain? You might initially, but eventually you'll pick up the phone and call a service repair man to fix it. That's where your mentor and coaches come in. The truly street savvy and successful individuals don't wait for their system to break down and give them problems. They do regular maintenance and checkups.

So, what are you, a thermometer or a thermostat? Which one do you want to be, and what's your temperature set at??

Coming to the realization that I am in direct control of my life and state of mind is probably the most important insight I have ever had in my life.

One of the biggest reasons people don't achieve what they want in life (and there are a few) is that they haven't mastered the ability to control the most important part of themselves—their state.

Your state, or your mental process, is really your mood at any given time, and your mood is emotional in nature. Think about the times when you're in a great fired-up mood. Think about how productive you are. Your focus and concentration are lasered to hit whatever you desire. The hard work and the speed bumps that come up don't matter; however, if you get yourself in a bad mood or even a neutral mood, it's highly unlikely you'll be willing to push yourself to greater heights.

A great quote, from one of my favorite movies, is by Jack Nicholson, in *The Departed*: "*I don't want to be a product of my environment; I want my environment to be a product of me.*"

Surprisingly, it's easier than you think to control your states. At first, it might seem daunting, like most new things, but the rewards you get will be far beyond what you could imagine. This is something I believe should be taught in every public education system in the world.

Now, to control your mental state, you need to have complete control of your physical state. Most people aren't aware that there is a strong body/mind connection that you can tap into.

The effects of this are obvious at first. For example, if you are torn up emotionally, what happens? You cry, you curl into a ball, you slouch your shoulders, your head bends down, or all the above. Now, try to make your body physically do the opposite of all that. Smile, do jumping jacks, stand up tall, with your head raised. How does that feel? Probably a lot better.

That's why exercise is such an important aspect of a happy, successful lifestyle. Getting regular exercise and physical activity not only keeps you in good health, it gives you more control over different aspects of your body.

What I find after a good workout is that my adrenaline is pumping like anything, which gives me more energy and makes me more alert.

A simple technique that Tony Robbins uses in a lot of his seminars is just a *Power Stance*. All you do is place your body like how I just described, which looks like a Superman or Peter Pan pose. Once there, hold the position for a minimum of 2 minutes, taking deep, long breaths from your diaphragm, and smiling. You will be shocked what this does to your mental state.

These theories have been backed by scientific studies. It has been found that when the body moves in certain ways, even the simple movement of smiling can cause the release of positive endorphins, which interact with receptors in the brain, and reduce the perception of pain and trigger positive feelings in the body, similar to that of Morphine.

The power stance has also been found to lower the primary stress hormone, Cortisol. This hormone is naturally produced in the body but has the unfortunate effect of increasing blood sugar levels, which affects weight gain, blood pressure, and obesity. It can also interfere with learning and memory.

The next thing to be aware of when trying to take command of your physical and mental state is, hands down, your diet. What you eat is so important to a healthy mental state and, unfortunately, our society is inundated with so much garbage food.

Studies are finding that a lot of the mental illnesses, such as ADHD, Alzheimer's, dementia, anxiety, and depression, have been strongly linked to excess sugar, food additives, and vegetable oils, while also being deficient in Omega-3 fatty acids.

Even foods such as processed meats and dairy are now being linked to chronic illnesses such as osteoporosis and different types of cancers.

The rule of thumb I have found is when figuring out what to eat, I stop and think whether the food was created naturally or created by man. For example, did nature create a Twinkie? No, man did that. Did nature create broccoli? Yes, so I can eat that.

Now, I'm not vegetarian, as I eat lots of chicken, eggs, and wild salmon. Around 80% of my diet is plant based.

When seeking out foods that are specifically good for your mind, stick to items such as blueberries, leafy greens (kale and spinach), walnuts, avocados, the spice turmeric, salmon, dark chocolate, broccoli, and of course, good old water. These items should be added to any grocery list for anyone that wants to have a specific benefit to mental health and development.

Other than that, I personally take a good multi-vitamin and a few Omega-3 capsules daily. Omega-3 fatty acids, EPA and DHA, are found in certain fish, but several studies have linked a higher intake of these healthy fats to decreased age-related mental decline and a reduced risk of Alzheimer's disease.

Additionally, another study found that people who eat fatty fish tend to have more gray matter in the brain. This is the brain tissue that processes information, memories, and emotions.

Overall, with this talk of exercise and diet, the best mental exercise you could be doing to achieve physical and financial success in life is by strengthening your vision and setting goals.

Having a strong vision is a common trait among successful people. The idea is that you should have a strong mental image of how you want your life to be. Where do you want to live? Who do you want to spend your time with? How is your typical day? All these things should clearly be seen in specific detail in your mind. This is your destination, your end point—what all the hard work is for.

Goal setting is a concept that's taught by pretty much every success guru around, and of course, every successful corporation on the planet has their own method for setting goals. If your vision is the destination, then goals are your GPS map to get there.

There are a lot of different ways of creating and writing out goals, but the method I use most often is the **SMART** approach.

SMART is an acronym that stands for the follow: **S** – Specific, **M** – Measurable, **A** – Achievable, **R** – Realistic, and **T** – Time.

The first letter, **S,** is for ***Specific***. Most people fail to achieve their goals, or any goal of value, due to a lack of specificity.

I used to train sales agents to sell products door to door. The most common question I would ask agents in the morning meeting was, "How many sales are you doing today?" A lot of them would respond with, "I dunno," or, "A couple." This, of course, was too vague. The agents who were specific and had a single number in mind, such as, "I'm getting 10 sales today," ended up being more successful. Even if the agent didn't hit their target, they typically always had higher results than the other agents that didn't.

The next letter, **M,** is for **Measurable**. A goal always needs to be measurable for you to see improvement. For example, if someone set the goal of "I want to be happier in life." To be honest, that's a nice thought, but how does one measure happiness? Plus, I could just buy you lunch, and that would make you at least a little happier, so then you'd be done. The best way to measure a goal is against a numerical value. Instead of saying, "I want to be happier," a better goal might be, "I will exercise at least 3 times per week, an hour per session." This goal has something that can now be measured, and the side effect, of course, is that when you hit this goal consistently, you will be happier.

A is for **Achievable**. Having a goal that you know you can achieve, is imperative. If I set a goal to be a trillionaire, this would be nice, but no one in the history of mankind has done it yet. By setting a goal that is not achievable, I will not have the mental stamina to keep at it. The better thing would be to set a long-term goal of being a billionaire. I know there are currently, as of this writing, 2,208 billionaires in the world. Now, if someone else has done it, then there's a possibility I can do it as well, and when I hit billionaire status, I could then reset my goals and seek being a trillionaire to push myself.

The next letter is **R,** for **Realistic**. Of course, your goals must be realistic. If I set a goal to be the CEO of a fortune 500 company by next Thursday, the chances of that happening are slim. In time, I could be in that position, but I would have to set lower goals that worked up to the main one within a certain amount of time.

This brings me to the last letter of **T**, for **Time**. All goals need to be measured in a length of time. Goals can and should be set for hourly, daily, weekly, monthly, yearly, and even in decades. Doing this will give you feedback on how you are doing, and gives you a deadline to push towards.

Now, setting your average goals are great, but I want you to do and achieve more. A good way to do this is to add another level and set a **Stretch Smart goal**. A stretch goal is exactly how it sounds. It's a goal that stretches you to new levels and new heights, while applying the same smart principles.

If you have a goal, for example, of earning $100,000 income per year, and your average income has been $50,000 thus far, this would be looked at as an average set goal. If, however, you truly wanted to stretch yourself, set your goal to earn $500,000 per year. If this is a little scary or daunting to you, good; it's supposed to be. The idea is that you want to push yourself farther than you have ever expected.

Don't worry about how you're going to achieve the goal. The most important thing is to set it and focus daily on it. The goal should be something that inspires and motivates you to achieve more. Sit and think of a goal that would really get you fired up and motivated about achieving, and shoot for that.

Keep in mind that the goal needs to be extremely attractive to you, as you will need that motivation to keep you going through all the ups and downs to get the desired outcome.

T. Harv Eker, who wrote the book, *Secrets of the Millionaire Mind*, says— "If you do what is hard, life will be easy; if you do what is easy, life will be hard."

The way to look at stretch goals is like driving on a highway. At first, it's almost scary traveling that fast and pushing your car's engine up to 120km an hour. After a short while, you get used to it. Now, what's interesting is when you come off the highway and go back into a 60km zone; it feels as if the car is going very slow from your new perception.

This is the benefit to stretching yourself with these goals. Once stretched, it's hard to go back to your original state.

This is part of the reason most wealthy people have a habit of regaining all their wealth if they mess up or go bankrupt. The truly successful know what they need to do to regain wealth. There's a theory that even if you took away all the wealth from everyone around the world and equally distributed it, within a short time, those people who were originally wealthy would have it all back, and the poor would be poor again. Not because they're bad and take advantage, but because they know the game.

Exercise #11

Create a list of Stretch SMART goals. Commit to and write down at least 3 goals for the areas of finance, health, and your relationships you want to improve. Remember when writing a goal to apply the smart principles to each one. Once you have your goals, stretch them a little farther than you think you could achieve. If you need any help writing out your goals, go to **www.moneymagnetpath.com.** There you'll find a page in the book bonuses section, of sample goals, and a goal writing sheet for you to keep them organized. From there, always keep your goals with you and constantly look at them. This will keep them fresh in your mind.

W.I.N.Ks

_____

_____

_____

_____

_____

_____

_____

_____

_____

_____

_____

_____

_____

_____

Chapter 12
Time to Give Back

*"Thousands of candles can be lighted from a single candle,
and the life of the candle will not be shortened.
Happiness never decreases by being shared."*
– Buddha

Well, you've made it to the end. You need to take a moment and congratulate yourself. You are now one of the few who *does*, as opposed to the many who just talk. Keep in mind that approximately 75% of people will never read a book after they leave the formal education system. It's a sad statistic, but one I think you and I can change.

This book really is just a stepping stone to a greater world of success and happiness for you and your family. What I really want to instill in you is what true wealth is. Wealth is the ability to live life on your terms. Go where you want, be with whom you want, and have want you want, when you want it. It's possible, and I know you can achieve it.

You see, nobody really wants money. People say they do, but the idea of having little plastic pieces of paper with deceased notables isn't really appealing. People want the feelings they associate with money—freedom, happiness, and love.

When you sit down and think about it, money isn't even a thing. I mean, it has been decades since currency was attached to any resource, such as gold. Money is an idea; it's a firm agreement backed by confidence and trust.

Let me explain: if I tell you that I am going to offer some sort of service for exchange of monetary value, then the only way you will agree to that is if there is some sort of confidence backing it. For example, if I pitch you an idea for a new investment and say it may work or may not work, you're unlikely to invest with me as I have no confidence.

However, if I give you the exact same idea and say with conviction it will work, and I give you all the pros and cons, with the reasons to why it will work, you're more than likely to invest. So, the true path to wealth is to gain agreement from as many people as possible, and back it with supreme confidence.

Now, don't get me wrong; I'm not saying you should go around lying to people. To be successful, you also need to maintain a high level of integrity, or it's all for nothing. Successful people take risks, but they take calculated risks that will minimize the downside. By doing this, they save themselves if things go bad but leave the upside to be pretty much limitless.

When Sir Richard Branson started Virgin Atlantic Airlines, everyone thought he was insane, as the airline industry is known to be very difficult with tight margins, and he was competing mainly against the long-standing company, British Airways. Branson was able to cut a deal that allowed him to return the planes should the company not have been successful. This allowed him to get into the airline industry with little downside and a huge amount of upside.

With the advent of internet marketing, the world has changed and allowed more new and curious ways for individuals to gain wealth by connecting everyone. The question is, will you take advantage or just let it slip by? So, go out there, get agreement, get trust, and be confident about it.

The most obvious piece of advice I can give you is that toys don't bring happiness. I think you know this, but I just wanted to reiterate. It's not what you have; it's what you become that makes you happy.

You can't bring the fancy car, the big screen tv, or the flashy house with you when you die. Creating lasting memories with the ones you love will bring you so much more joy in your life.

Because of this, I've learned to love traveling. In the last two years alone, I've taken my family to Paris, the Caribbean, and Ecuador. This year, we will be heading to Venice, Mexico, and Florida. It has given us greater connection and lasting memories that my children will cherish. The cultural expansion has also helped my daughters, as they are now on their way to being tri-lingual at the age of 5.

The real benefit to being wealthy is that you now have removed a large barrier that prevents you from being with your family—never forget that.

Probably the biggest misconception with wealth is that you must work a tremendous number of hours and sacrifice your health and your family to make it. Initially, you may need to make some sacrifices, but I don't want that for you or me, and I wouldn't promote wealth if it did.

Sure, you can make *money* by doing that, but that's not the goal of this book. It's to be able to have your money make more money, eliminate financial stresses, and give you the free time you deserve.

The next idea that will help you to feel satisfied and give your life purpose is to live for something beyond yourself and give back. Pretty much every religious text and a multitude of self-help books preach the benefits to tithing and donating to charity.

This act alone can create positive feelings within you to have accomplishment and feel like you are a true benefit to the human race.

The typical idea is to donate or tithe 10% of your net income, but in time, that amount could be higher. If you have a hard time donating, start off small. Even donating clothes or stuff around your home you don't use anymore could be a good start and may help someone less fortunate. It'll probably also free up extra space around the house.

It was reported in February 2018 that Bill Gates and his wife, Melinda's, charitable organization, The Gates Foundation, founded along with fellow billionaire, Warren Buffet, will be donating most of his 90-billion-dollar fortune over their lifetime, and even after death.

According to Bill, in a letter released, it comes down to two reasons: The work is both meaningful and fun. He states, *"Even before we got married, we talked about how we would eventually spend a lot of time on philanthropy. We think that's a basic responsibility of anyone with a lot of money. Once you've taken care of yourself and your children, the best use of extra wealth is to give it back to society."*

So, think about what and how you can help a great cause, and how you can continue helping mankind before and after death.

Now, the final note I would like to bring up in this book is that it is far from being a complete financial textbook. The concepts in this book are explained simplistically and are the groundwork for a much larger world. The financial industry is massive and always changing, so as I said earlier, this is the end but also the beginning.

From here, I would hope you continue your financial education for yourself and your family. You owe it to them. If you want to be financially independent, then it will take a bit of prep work. Abraham Lincoln said, *"If I had one hour to chop down a tree, I'd spend the first forty minutes sharpening my axe."* This is true, as success is when opportunity meets preparation.

You might think that some of the concepts are too hard or too complicated. Well, living in poverty is a lot harder (trust me, I've been there). If you don't understand something, find someone who does, and learn from them. Take courses, and go to seminars and workshops. I currently read at least three new books a month, and hope to increase that to four.

Learning to speed read can be a huge asset, so I recommend taking a speed-reading course or registering for one online. I personally took and recommend Jim Kwik's speed reading and memory course, at **www.kwiklearningonline.com**. Just note, I do not receive any bonuses or commissions from recommending Jim; I just really respect his work.

Life is about learning and growth—and remember, leaders are readers—so to help, I have added a few books to start you off that I recommend. All these books had drastic benefits to how I view life and finances.

Further Recommended Reading on Success and Financial Literacy:

Napoleon Hill, *Think and Grow Rich:* (The Ralson Society, 1937)
T. Harv Eker, *Secrets of the Millionaire Mind:* (HarperCollins, 2005)
Bob Proctor, *You Were Born Rich:* (Life Success Productions; Reprint ed. 1997)
Ray Dalio, *Principles:* (Simon & Schuster, 2017)
Raymond Aaron, *Double Your Income Doing What You Love:* (Wiley, 2008)
George S. Clason, *The Richest Man in Babylon*: (CreateSpace Independent Publishing Platform, 2016)
Timothy Ferris*, The 4-Hour Work Week:* (Harmony, 2009)
Robert T. Kiyosaki, *Rich Dad, Poor Dad:* (Plata Publishing, 2017)
David Chilton, *The Wealthy Barber:* (Stoddart Publishing, 1995)
Tony Robbins, *Awaken the Giant Within:* (Free Press, 1992)
Dale Carnegie, *How to Win Friends & Influence People:* (Gallery Books, Revised ed. 1998)
Victor E. Frankl, *Man's Search for Meaning:* (Beacon Press, 2006)

And just about any autobiography on successful people.

So, my final thought to you before you finish: There will be ups, there will be downs, but as the hockey legend, Wayne Gretzky, says, *"You miss 100% of the shots you don't take."*

I came from a low-income family, and by any means I didn't have any other benefits to my life. All I had was my health and a driving attitude to do and be more. I now am happy to say I am financially independent, have a loving wife, and two beautiful daughters whom I adore.

I have made mistakes along the way, and that's normal. It's how you learn from these mistakes that makes you better for the next challenge.

A great analogy I learned was from the great speaker, Les Brown, about the Chinese Bamboo tree. Most people don't know that it takes 5 years for that tree to grow. The thing is, you have to water and fertilize the seed every day for 5 years, or it won't grow. During that time, there is absolutely no change to the seed—nothing.

Then, one day, at year 5, that plant explodes in growth and shoots up to 9 feet tall within a six-week period. The question is then, does the plant grow in 6 weeks or 5 years? The answer is obvious. It grows for 5 years; you just can't see it.

So, see how this can relate to you. You can and probably will study and develop for a time with no change. It happened to me. Don't let it discourage you. Eventually, with the effort and seeds you put in, you will reap a harvest greater than you can ever imagine. Everyone has the same potential for greatness.

Thomas Jefferson said, *"If you want something you've never had before, you'll need to do something you've never done before."* Life is a gift; don't have regrets. God Bless.

W.I.N.Ks

About the Author

Ryan Baily is an award-winning author, international public speaker, and peak performance coach. He was born and raised in Guelph, Ontario, but currently lives in Brampton, Ontario, Canada with his wife and 2 daughters. He is currently licenced in Canadian provinces for life insurance and mutual fund products.

The author is available for speeches to appropriate audiences, as well as private coaching sessions. For rates and availability, please contact the author directly at RyanBaily@moneymagnetpath.com.

For a free financial analysis in the Canadian marketplace, feel free to contact the author at RBaily10nenc@wfgmail.ca.

To order more books, please visit www.amazon.com.

Finally, if you have been inspired or motivated by any portion of this book, the best thing you could do is share that new knowledge and be someone's guiding light. The world needs more candles to light the way of others.